ECHOES
FROM
WALDEN

POEMS INSPIRED BY THOREAU'S LIFE AND WORK

ECHOES
FROM
WALDEN

POEMS INSPIRED BY THOREAU'S LIFE AND WORK

EDITED BY DAVID K. LEFF

WAYFARER BOOKS
WWW.WAYFARERBOOKS.COM
AN IMPRINT OF HOMEBOUND PUBLICATIONS

© 2021 DAVID K. LEFF

Wayfarer Books supports copyright. Copyright fuels creativity, encourages diverse voices, promotes free speech, and creates a vibrant culture. Thank you for buying an authorized edition of this book and for complying with copyright laws by not reproducing, scanning, or distributing any part of it in any form without permission. You are supporting writers and allowing Wayfarer Books to continue to publish for every reader.

All Rights Reserved
Published in 2021 by Wayfarer Books
Cover Design and Interior Design by Leslie M. Browning
PBK 978-1-0880-0438-8
Cover Image © Walden Pond by Naya Dadara
Herbert W. Gleason photographs used courtesy
of the Walden Woods Project, Lincoln, Massachusetts
Frontispiece: Walden Pond from House Site
p.1: Walden Early Winter | p. 6: Concord River June
p. 21: Walden Pond Winter | p. 40: River Fog | p. 75: Baker Farm

10 9 8 7 6 5 4 3 2 1

Homebound Publications and its imprints, are committed to ecological stewardship. We greatly value the natural environment and invest in environmental conservation. For each book purchased in our online store we plant one tree.

CONTENTS

xi   Acknowledgements

xv   Brag and Exaggeration: A Foreword
       by Jeffrey S. Cramer

xvii   Introduction: When the Poetic Frenzy Seizes Us
       by David K. Leff

Speaking for Himself

3   Henry David Thoreau, "I am a parcel of vain strivings tied"
5   Henry David Thoreau, "My life is the poem I would have writ"

Friends & Contemporaries

11   A. Bronson Alcott, "Sonnet XIII"
12   Ralph Waldo Emerson, "Forbearance"
13   Daniel Ricketson, "Thoreau's Cairn"
15   William Ellery Channing, "Walden"
17   James Russell Lowell, *from*, "A Fable for Critics"
18   Franklin B. Sanborn, "Thoreau"
19   Louisa May Alcott, "Thoreau's Flute"

Within Living Memory and Beyond

27   Katherine Tynan, "Thoreau at Walden"
29   William Butler Yeats, "The Lake Isle of Innisfree"
30   Odell Shepard, "The Grave of Thoreau"
32   Florence Kiper Frank, "Thoreau"
33   Edmund Wilson, "The Extravert at Walden Pond"
35   Isadore Elizabeth Flanders, "To Thoreau"
36   Paul Engle, "Henry David Thoreau"
37   Howard Nutt, "Thoreau"

Inspirations Further into the Twentieth Century

43   William Bronk, "Flowers, the World and My Friend, Thoreau"
46   Maxine Kumin, "Beans"
48   Robert Francis, "Thoreau in Italy"
50   Tomas Tranströmer, "Five Stanzas to Thoreau"
52   Donald Junkins, "July"
54   Milton Kessler, "The Good Death: for Henry David Thoreau a Century Later"
55   Charles Tidler, "Transcending the Sublime Henry David"
58   Barry Targan, "Thoreau Stalks the Land Disguised as a Father"
60   Hai Zi (Zha Haisheng), "Thoreau Has Brains"
64   Parkman Howe, "Letter from Wachusett"
69   John Enright, "Teaching Thoreau"
70   Barry Sternlieb, "Thoreau's Hat"
72   Timothy Liu, "Thoreau"
73   Edward Morin, "Labor Day at Walden Pond"

Third Century Voices

- 81 Mary Oliver, "Going to Walden"
- 82 Aaron Silverberg, "Thoreau's Chair"
- 83 Charlie Mehrhoff, "Spring Birdlife"
- 84 J. Walter Brain, "The Loon at Walden"
- 85 Ingela Strandberg, "Dear Mr. Thoreau!"
- 86 David Starkey, "Allen Ginsberg in Thoreau's Maine Woods"
- 88 John Kinsella, "Sacred Kingfisher and Trough Filled with Water Pumped from Deep Underground"
- 90 Ian Marshall, "Higher Laws"
- 92 David Wagoner, "Thoreau and the Lightning"
- 93 L.M. Browning, "On the Far Side of Walden"
- 95 Cammy Thomas, "Refraction"
- 96 Todd Davis, "Thoreau Casts a Line in the Merrimack"
- 97 Susan Blackwell Ramsey, "How to Seduce Henry David Thoreau"
- 99 Gene G. Bradbury, "Lament"
- 100 Cecily Parks, "When I was Thoreau at Night"
- 102 Corinne Hosfeld Smith, "Notes on Thoreau's Notes from Mackinac Island"
- 104 Amy Nawrocki, "The Charity Houses of Cape Cod"
- 107 Ginny Lowe Connors, "Thoreau's Pumpkins"
- 109 Alison Croggon, "Sonnet: Thoreau in Chernobyl"
- 110 David K. Leff, "Vain Strivings Untied"
- 112 Janice Miller Potter, "Thoreau's Umbrella"
- 114 John Reibetanz, "Thoreau's Pencils"

Notes on Contributors

Notes on Texts and Credits

Appendix: Selected Additional Poems About Thoreau

ACKNOWLEDGEMENTS

My deepest gratitude to Jeffrey S. Cramer, Curator of Collections at the Walden Woods Project's Thoreau Institute Library, for his tireless support and invaluable advice and assistance, including use of the library and hosting my first presentation of this project in its incipient stages.

The Thoreau Society and its executive director, Michael Frederick, have my undying appreciation for inviting me to present poetry about Thoreau at the 2019 Annual Gathering. Special thanks to James Finley and members of the Thoreau Society Fellowship Committee for awarding me the 2019 Marjorie Harding Memorial Fellowship enabling me to pursue this anthology.

Thanks also to Erin Monahan for research assistance and help transcribing poems, Frederick Courtright of The Permissions Company for his diligent efforts to obtain the rights to many of the works in this volume, Julia Du who translated and obtained the rights to Hai Zi's wonderful poem, Corinne H. Smith, supervisor of the Thoreau Society Shop at Walden Pond, for her early and continued encouragement, and to Leslie Browning, publisher extraordinaire, who saw value in this project from the first and enthusiastically helped move it forward.

A special shout-out to Henrik Otterberg, Thoreau Society board member and expert bibliographic compiler for the *Thoreau Society Bulletin*, for his generosity of spirit, sharing his vast knowledge of writings about Thoreau, and fine translations of poems by Tomas Tranströmer and Ingela Strandberg. Without his diligent efforts, this book would not have been possible.

I'm also grateful to the many poets and publishers who contributed work, especially those who agreed to have poems appear gratis. Without them, there would be no anthology. I have scrutinized the final rendition as best I can. If there are errors, I apologize and acknowledge full responsibility.

I greatly appreciate the Walden Woods Project for use of the classic Thoreau Country photographs of Herbert W. Gleason (1855-1937). Gleason made extensive study of Thoreau's writings and explored the places Thoreau wrote about. His photographs have illustrated Thoreau's works since 1906.

Lastly, but certainly not least, I am forever grateful to my wife, Mary C. Fletcher, for her interest and patience as she likely achieved the world's record for hearing the most poems about Thoreau read aloud.

BRAG AND EXAGGERATION

A Foreword by Jeffrey S. Cramer
Curator of Collections at the Walden Woods Project's Thoreau Institute Library

HENRY DAVID THOREAU. You either love him or you hate him. He invokes passion. Very few can simply take him or leave him. Those who admire him do so almost to distraction, and those who don't spew venom. Most of the poets collected here are from the first group. They found profound inspiration, something transformative, and—dare I use the word? —transcendental in the words of this mid-19th century American author.

In the process each poet has perhaps created a mythic or heroic figure, a Thoreau who may never have walked the streets of Concord, but who lives and breathes and walks in their minds. These poets are portraits artists, not daguerreotypists. If these writers can, Thoreau wrote,

> return a man's life more perfect to our hands, than it was left at his death, following out the design of its author, we shall have no great cause to complain. We do not want a Daguerreotype likeness... If these virtues were not in this man, perhaps they are in his biographer,—no fatal mistake. Really, in any other sense, we never do, nor desire to, come at the historical man, — unless we rob his grave ...

And that's what poets do. Poetry, Thoreau said, "is in one sense an infinite brag & exaggeration." Here is the brag and the exaggeration, from his contemporaries to ours, all coming from "the imagination of poets" — that place from where, according to Thoreau, they put "brave speeches into the mouths of their heroes."

Thoreau knew that it was "hard to read a contemporary poet critically … We go within the fane of the temple and hear the faint music of the worshippers, but posterity will have to stand without and consider the vast proportions and grandeur of the building." And this these poets have magnificently done, considering from varying perspectives the vastness and the grandeur while speaking a truth that Thoreau would have appreciated.

To paraphrase Thoreau,

>   These poems are the life he would have writ,
>   Could he have both lived and uttered it.

INTRODUCTION

When the Poetic Frenzy Seizes Us
by David K. Leff

There are American writers better known and more widely read than Henry David Thoreau, but few are as beloved by his fans. Many readers and aficionados refer to him by the familiar "Henry," as if he was a family member or a dear friend. Beyond just admiring and respecting his genius, Thoreau is cherished.

Why this deep affection for a man who could be a bit prickly, save in the company of children? Something in his work seems to touch us personally. When I was a teenager, his defiance of social norms had great appeal for me. As I grew older, I was invigorated by his sense of social justice as an abolitionist, and by his call for non-violent resistance to immoral government action. His critique of society's complications and the folly of wealth grows more meaningful as time goes on and life becomes increasingly material and frenetic. His delight in walking, wild places, and the inspiring power of nature has only become more pertinent and vibrant as development and technology proceed apace. All Thoreauvians have their reasons, often ones that resonate deeply and individually. There is a Thoreau for all seasons of the year and all seasons of life— he was literally a man for all seasons, if ever there was one. Perhaps it is this emotional attachment that yields poems.

As my reading of poetry widened over time, I kept stumbling on poems about Thoreau. At first, I didn't give it much thought, but they kept adding up. Why, I wondered, did poets, those artists of compressed, impactful, and often emotional expression, continue to write about him without pause from his time to ours? What were these poems saying about Thoreau and our relationship to him? How did impressions and expressions change over the decades?

I quickly learned that more poems had been written *about* Thoreau than he'd ever written himself. But, as my reading persisted with a purpose, it soon seemed that no other individual had inspired so many poems by such a variety of authors, with the exception perhaps of religious figures. As I continued to encounter and enjoy Thoreau poems, it occurred to me that devotees and scholars of Thoreau might benefit from a collection of them.

What, I wondered, would an anthology of Thoreau poems tell us about the meaning of his work and our aspirations for a better world? There are biographies, essay collections, volumes probing his interest in nature, social justice, science and a plethora of other topics, both obvious and obscure. In fact, he's become a brand, a name that increasingly resonates in these times of growing challenges for the natural world, cluttered lives, and ever enlarging government and corporate presences. Yet, there are no collections of verse about him.

In a summer 1970 issue of the *Thoreau Society Bulletin* in which he discussed nineteenth century poems, Robert F. Stowell estimated that a complete catalog of poems about Thoreau might come to more than 300. Throw in the late twentieth and early twenty-first centuries and the total may easily approach twice that number. It's likely an exhaustive list may never be compiled since there's an ever-expanding universe of new poems, and ones from the past continue to be discovered in libraries, attics, and in old newspapers and magazines. No doubt there is a lot of Thoreau-energized nature poetry that will never be traced back to the Concord naturalist.

Of course, while a remarkable constellation of Thoreau poems sparkle with insight and poetic craft, not all are of equal merit. Although opinions on poems are somewhat subjective, it's clear that by any measure some are not very good. Stowell raised this issue when he noted that "mawkish sentimentality and excessive adulation are the most frequent faults, followed by a narrow understanding of Thoreau and a tendency to paraphrase from his own writing." Turning an evocatively poetic phrase himself, he observed that the worst ones "sweep up to 'Dear Henry' with a bouquet while trying to clutch his trouser leg."

Although no anthology of Thoreau poems has ever been published, the notion of collecting poems about him is not new. Leading twentieth century Thoreau scholar and inveterate collector of Thoreauviana, Walter Harding, accumulated a thick file of poems among his various books and artifacts. Now safely ensconced at the Thoreau Institute Library, curator Jeffery Cramer eagerly shared the trove. Many of the poems I'd never seen. They ranged from work that had appeared in leading publications like *The New Yorker*, to pieces handwritten on scraps of notebook paper.

Thoreau aspired to be a poet, but his greatest poetry was in his life, not his stanzas. "The true poem is the poet's mind" wrote Thoreau's friend and mentor Ralph Waldo Emerson. Thoreau translated that into regular outpourings of words in his voluminous journal. "Is not the poet bound to write his own biography?" he queried on the afternoon of October 21, 1857. "Is there any other work for him but in a good journal? We do not wish to know how his imaginary hero, but how he, the actual hero, lived from day to day." Thoreau wrote relatively few poems and they are hardly as well-known as his essays. But how he could make prose sing—with poetic rhythm and vivid images. On his own terms, he lived at the apex of poetry. So, perhaps it's fitting for a man who saw a life well lived as a form of poetry that there be poems written about his life.

Thoreau found poetry in all aspects of living, even in surveying and scientific inquiry. Afloat on the Concord River near Chelmsford with his brother in 1839, he consulted a gazetteer and "from its bald natural facts extracted the pleasure of poetry." Thoreau's abiding love of verse, even as he became increasingly precise in his nature studies, indicates an important tie between right and left-brain pursuits that gave him a sense of wholeness, a connection for which many of us long. This is the loadstone of creative thought. Perhaps it's this confluence of thinking which, in part, makes his writing so compelling.

Poetry about Thoreau may be critical to understanding his image and reputation by environmentalists, literary scholars, historians, social activists, philosophers, and others. Poems concerning his life, work, and philosophy are written by people from all walks of life and of various literary and professional talents. Beginning in Thoreau's lifetime, they illustrate our changing views of the man in a heartfelt form of expression with a high specific gravity, a density of feeling and meaning.

As Thoreau's reputation grows and changes from interest by likeminded contemporaries to late nineteenth century conservationists and woodsman, to independent living proponents in the Great Depression, and social justice and environmental advocates in the 1960s and 1970s, we find poetic interpretations of Thoreau changing. These often reflect as much, if not more about us as a society than they do about Thoreau's life and philosophy.

The universe of Thoreau poems ranges from rhymed metrical work to free verse, from sensual experiences of nature to philosophical musings. There are haiku, prose poems, sonnets, and even a limerick that would not make a shy person blush. Some appear in books, newspapers and magazines, others remain in typescript or are handwritten. They are penned by poets whose names are well known, and many more that are obscure. Regardless, each poet has been moved by Thoreau to make a creative statement.

As much as I'd be delighted putting together a comprehensive volume, such a book would not only be unmanageable, but by necessity incomplete as new poems are discovered or written. Selecting the fifty or so poems for this volume proved to be a difficult and disagreeable task as I had to leave out many incisive and beautiful pieces. Why fifty? Maybe because the bulk of the work occurred during the fiftieth anniversary of Earth Day. It's as good a reason as any. Why a few more than fifty? I couldn't help myself. Even so, many deserving poets and poems did not make it between these covers. Perhaps the supplemental list of poems in the appendix will compensate a little for my sins of omission. Failure to appear within these pages is no judgment on the merits of work not included.

Certainly, the subject of all this verse should have his say, so the selections begin with two autobiographical poems by Thoreau, the only poet permitted more than one. Next up are his contemporaries, mostly fond reminiscences by friends, some of whom elevate him to myth. Louisa May Alcott calls him "Pan" and William Ellery Channing describes him as "a holy man."

Presented in rough chronology following Thoreau's contemporaries, there's a grouping of poems written from the late 1800s into the early 1900s, then another cohort from the balance of the twentieth century, and a fair-sized final cluster from the twenty-first illustrating the accelerating number of such poems being written and published.

Among the poets, are well known authors of many books who have appeared in leading journals and magazines. They include a poet laureate of the United States, Pulitzer Prize winners, National Book Award Winners, and Nobel laureates. They are joined by less well-known published poets who also write in beautifully compelling ways, capturing the Thoreauvian spirit. Nine of the poets are from outside the United States, three of whom required translation into English.

The poems include epistolary messages and conversations with Henry, imaginative works that conjure Thoreau as the writer's companion in various times and places, mini biographies, and contemplations on Thoreau's time at Walden. Some poets make pilgrimages to the pond, write about encounters with Thoreauvian nature, or focus on social justice and independent living. There are even playful satirical poems like James Russell Lowell's "Fable for Critics" and Edmund Wilson's "The Extravert at Walden Pond." It seems there is a different Thoreau for every poetic style and sensibility.

What do the poems tell us about Thoreau? What do they say about ourselves and our connection to the man; his philosophy; and his evocative, impassioned, and often surprisingly humorous style of writing? Do they offer insight into Thoreau's impact on our culture? Every reader may take away different notions, but no one is likely to turn these pages without some enlightenment.

Can poetry say something that has not already been rendered in prose? Perhaps poems add nothing substantively, but are probative on a noncognitive, intuitive, gut level of sensation and empathic exploration. More than any footnoted prose, it may help explain why Thoreau's legacy is both enduring and endearing.

Poems about Thoreau have been written in every generation since his time. They are scattered like so many colorful autumn leaves blown about by the wind. Here some are gathered together in a pile that will compost in the minds of readers and yield a rich humus, fertile soil that will sprout interest in Thoreau's work and inspire generations to come.

Speaking for Himself

*I have frequently seen a poet withdraw,
having enjoyed the most valuable part of a farm,
while the crusty farmer supposed
that he had got a few wild apples only.*
—Walden

HENRY DAVID THOREAU

I am a parcel of vain strivings tied

I am a parcel of vain strivings tied
    By a chance bond together,
   Dangling this way and that, their links
     Were made so loose and wide,
        Methinks,
     For milder weather.

A bunch of violets without their roots,
    And sorrel intermixed,
  Encircled by a wisp of straw
    Once coiled about their shoots,
      The law
    By which I'm fixed.

A nosegay which Time clutched from out
    Those fair Elysian fields,
 With weeds and broken stems, in haste,
    Doth make the rabble rout
      That waste
    The day he yields.

And here I bloom for a short hour unseen,
    Drinking my juices up,
  With no root in the land
    To keep my branches green,
      But stand
    In a bare cup.

Some tender buds were left upon my stem
    In mimicry of life,
  But ah! the children will not know,
    Till time has withered them,
      The woe
        With which they're rife.

But now I see I was not plucked for naught,
    And after in life's vase
  Of glass set while I might survive,
    But by a kind hand brought
      Alive
        To a strange place.

That stock thus thinned will soon redeem its hours,
    And by another year,
  Such as God knows, with freer air,
    More fruits and fairer flowers
      Will bear,
        While I droop here.

HENRY DAVID THOREAU
My life has been the poem I would have writ

My life has been the poem I would have writ,
But I could not both live and utter it.

Friends & Contemporaries

*You might frequently say of a poet away from home
that he was as mute as a bird of passage,
uttering a mere chip from time to time,
but follow him to his true habitat,
and you shall not know him,
he will sing so melodiously.*
—Journal, March 25, 1858

A. BRONSON ALCOTT
Sonnet XIII

Who nearer Nature's life would truly come
Must nearest come to him of whom I speak;
He all kinds knew, — the vocal and the dumb;
Masterful in genius was he, and unique,
Patient, sagacious, tender, frolicsome.
This Concord Pan would oft his whistle take,
And forth from wood and fen, field, hill, and lake,
Trooping around him, in their several guise,
The shy inhabitants their haunts forsake:
Then he, like Esop, man would satirize,
Hold up the image wild to clearest view
Of undiscerning manhood's puzzled eyes,
And mocking say, "Lo! mirrors here for you:
Be true as these, if ye would be more wise."

RALPH WALDO EMERSON
Forbearance

Hast thou named all the birds without a gun?
Loved the wood-rose, and left it on its stalk?
At rich men's tables eaten bread and pulse?
Unarmed, faced danger with a heart of trust?
And loved so well a high behavior,
In man or maid, that thou from speech refrained,
Nobility more nobly to repay?
O, be my friend, and teach me to be thine!

DANIEL RICKETSON
Thoreau's Cairn

The friends of Thoreau now each drop a stone
Upon the place where stood his rustic cot,
To rear a monument unto his name
A simple mound to memory ever dear,
Such as the philosopher himself might choose.
Here in his early manhood came this man,
And built his cabin near his favorite pond,
Since known to thousands who his works admire
And venerate the soul to nature dear.
The stately wood then standing, and the pond,
Were his great source of study and resort,
Forgetting not his books of ancient lore
In winter's hours, or summer's sultry heat.
Here close to nature as her child he lived,
And found such wisdom from her simple store,
And made such record for the after-time,
That a large class of young ingenuous minds,
As well as older, now regard his works
Among the choicest of our noblest minds.
O! happy Concord, still the chosen home
Of wise and learned in poetry and prose,
Once friends of him who more than all the rest
Took up his darling Concord for his theme,
And brought his pictures for the public view.
This air he breathed, these scenes he loved as life;

No tree, nor shrub, nor bird, nor insect small,
Escaped his notice—all were dear to him,
And full of wise instruction. The pilgrim
Here with meditative steps may wander,
And learn from the works of this noble man
How much the common food of life affords
Of nurture to the seeking, thoughtful soul.
At nature's table all may fare alike;
She spreads her feast for all with loving eyes,
And feeds the soul with true, substantial bliss.
Then ever-sacred may this spot remain
To nature and her worshippers sincere
Who still can see an ever-present God
In all his works, and reverently adore.
O! may no sacrilegious hands disturb
Those haunts to virtue and to memory dear;
But in the after years let others come,
As we now come, and reverently place
A monumental stone unto his name.

WILLIAM ELLERY CHANNING
Walden

It is not far beyond the village church,
After we pass the wood that skirts the road,
A Lake,—the blue-eyed Walden, that doth smile
Most tenderly upon its neighbor Pines,
And they as if to recompense this love,
In double beauty spread their branches forth.
This Lake has tranquil loveliness and breadth,
And of late years has added to its charms,
For one attracted to its pleasant edge,
Has built himself a little Hermitage,
Where with much piety he passes life.

More fitting place I cannot fancy now,
For such a man to let the line run off
The mortal reel, such patience hath the lake,
Such gratitude and cheer is in the Pines.
But more than either lake or forest's depths,
This man has in himself; a tranquil man,
With sunny sides where well the fruit is ripe,
Good front, and resolute bearing to this life,
And some serener virtues, which control
This rich exterior prudence, virtues high,
That in the principles of Things are set,
Great by their nature and consigned to him,
Who, like a faithful merchant, does account

To God for what he spends, and in what way.
Thrice happy art thou, Walden! in thyself,
Such purity is in thy limpid springs;
In those green shores which do reflect in thee,
And in this man who dwells upon thy edge,
A holy man within a Hermitage.
May all good showers fall gently into thee,
May thy surrounding forests long be spared,
And may the Dweller on thy tranquil shores,
There lead a life of deep tranquillity
Pure as thy Waters, handsome as thy Shores
And with those virtues which are like the Stars.

JAMES RUSSELL LOWELL
from, A Fable for Critics

There comes_____, for instance; to see him's a rare sport,
Tread in Emerson's tracks with legs painfully short;
How he jumps, how he strains, and gets red in the face,
To keep step with the mystagogue's natural pace!
He follows as close as a stick to a rocket,
His fingers exploring the prophet's each pocket.
Fie, for shame, brother bard; with good fruit of your own,
Can't you let neighbor Emerson's orchards alone?
Besides, 'tis no use, you'll not find e'en a core, —
_____has picked up all the windfalls before.
They might stirp every tree, and E. never would catch 'em,
His Hesperides have no rude dragon to watch 'em;
When they send him a dishfull, and ask him to try 'em,
He never suspects how the sly rogues came by 'em;
He wonders why 'tis there are none such his trees on,
And thinks 'em the best he has tasted this season.

FRANKLIN B. SANBORN
Thoreau

Hush the loud chant, ye birds, at eve and morn,
    And something plaintive let the robin sing;
Gone is our Woodman, leaving us forlorn,
    And veiled with tears the merry face of Spring.
Our woods and pastures be for other groves
    Forsakes and wanders now by fairer streams;
Yet not forgetful of his earthly loves,—
    Ah, no! for so affection fondly dreams.
Dear One! 'Twere shame to weep above thy grave,
    Or doubtingly thy soul's far flight pursue;
Peace and Delight must there await the brave,
    And Love attend the loving, wise, and true.
Thy well-kept vows our broken aims shall mend,
    Oft as we think of thee, great–hearted friend!

LOUISA MAY ALCOTT
Thoreau's Flute

We, sighing, said, "Our Pan is dead;
His pipe hangs mute beside the river;—
Around his wistful sunbeams quiver,
But Music's airy voice is fled.
Spring mourns as for untimely frost;
The bluebird chants a requiem;
The willow-blossom waits for him;—
The Genius of the wood is lost."

Then from the flute, untouched by hands,
There came a low, harmonious breath:
"For such as he there is no death;—
His life the eternal life commands;
Above man's aims his nature rose:
The wisdom of a just content
Made one small spot a continent
And turned to poetry Life's prose.

"Haunting the hills, the stream, the wild,
Swallow and aster, lake and pine,
To him grew human or divine,—
Fit mates for this large-hearted child.
Such homage Nature ne'er forgets,
And yearly on the coverlid
'Neath which her darling lieth hid
Will write his name in violets.

"To him no vain regrets belong,
Whose soul, that finer instrument,
Gave to the world no poor lament,
But wood-notes ever sweet and strong.
O lonely friend! he still will be
A potent presence, though unseen,—
Steadfast, sagacious, and serene:
Seek not for him—he is with thee."

Within Living Memory and Beyond

The poet will prevail to be popular in spite of his faults, and in spite of his beauties too. He will hit the nail on the head, and we shall not know the shape of his hammer.
—A Week on the Concord and Merrimack Rivers

KATHARINE TYNAN
Thoreau at Walden

A little log-hut in the woodland dim,
A still lake, like a bit of summer sky,
On the glad heart of which great lilies lie.
"Ah!" he had said, "the Naiads, white of limb."
In those green glooms fair shapes did come to him,
He saw a Dryad's sheeny drapery
Shimmer at dusk, he heard Pan pipe hereby
A lusty strain to fauns and satyrs grim.
For that he was fair Nature's leal knight;
She loved him, taught him all her grammarye,
All the quaint secrets of her magic clime.
He heard the unborn flowers' springing footsteps light,
And the wind's whisper of the enchanted sea,
And the birds sing of love, and pairing-time.

II.

Seeking this sage in fair fraternity
Came Hawthorne here and Emerson, I know.
O happy woods, that watched them to and fro!
Thrice happy woods, that hearkened to the three!
Yet, my rare Thoreau! a thought comes to me
Of one sweet soul you missed, who long ago
Went through Assisi's streets, with eyes aglow
And worn meek face, and lips curved tenderly.

So for God's dumb things was this great heart stirred,
Called he the happy birds his sisters sweet,
The fish his brethren, blessed them, prayed with them.
Now, my sweet-hearted Pagan! had you heard,
You would have wept upon his wounded feet,
And craved a blessing from the hands of him.

William Butler Yeats
The Lake Isle of Innisfree

I will arise and go now, and go to Innisfree,
And a small cabin build there, of clay and wattles made:
Nine bean-rows will I have there, a hive for the honey-bee,
And live alone in the bee-loud glade.

And I shall have some peace there, for peace comes dropping slow,
Dropping from the veils of the morning to where the cricket sings;
There midnight's all a glimmer, and noon a purple glow,
And evening full of the linnet's wings.

I will arise and go now, for always night and day
I hear lake water lapping with low sounds by the shore;
While I stand on the roadway, or on the pavements grey,
I hear it in the deep heart's core.

ODELL SHEPARD
The Grave of Thoreau

Brown earth, blue sky, and solitude,—
Three things he loved, three things he wooed
Lifelong; and now no rhyme can tell
How ultimately all is well
With his wild heart that worshipped God's
Epiphany in crumbling sods
And like an oak brought all its worth
Back to the kindly mother earth.

But something starry, something bold,
Eludes the clutch of dark and mould,—
Something that will not wholly die
Out of the old familiar sky.
No spell in all the lore of graves
Can still the plash of Walden waves
Or wash away the azure stain
Of Concord skies from heart and brain.
Clear psalteries and faint citoles
Only recall the orioles
Fluting reveille to the morn
Across the acres of the corn.

He wanders somewhere lonely still
Along a solitary hill
And sits by ever lonelier fires
Remote from heaven's bright rampires.
A hermit in the blue Beyond
Beside some dim celestial pond
With beans to hoe and wood to hew
And halcyon days to loiter through
And angel visitors, no doubt,
Who shut the air and sunlight out.
But he who scoffed at human ways
And, finding us unworthy of praise,
Sang misanthropic paeans to
The muskrat and the feverfew,
Will droop those archangelic wings
With praise of how we manage things,
Prefer his Walden tupelo
To even the Tree of Life, and grow
A little wistful looking down
Across the fields of Concord town.

FLORENCE KIPER FRANK
Thoreau

After seeing Walden Pond

The green things in their growing knew his heart
As quick with budding impulse as their own.
The solitude had found a solitude
As wild and holy; the keen starlight knew
A gleam as keen and subtle; the high trees
Heavenward reaching, reached and yearned through him
And in his blood their living sap was quick.
The candor of the good brown earth he knew,
The wide simplicity of growing fields,
The mystery and rapture of the dawn
Shimmer and depth of his dear pond he held,
Shimmer and liquid depth, and glancing beams
of sunlight on its surface; these he knew
As in himself, this lover of the woods.

EDMUND WILSON
The Extravert at Walden Pond

To Betty Spencer, who said that somebody's statement that "Thoreau was a neuro" sounded like a song by Cole Porter.

A jumps-and-jitters fighter,
   As some of you may know,
Was the great American writer,
   Henry D. Thoreau.
He was skilled at making pencils
   And the neighbors bought his goods,
But he grabbed a few utensils
   And he vanished in the woods.

Oh, Thoreau was a neuro —
   Like us, you will admit.
He went without a bureau —
   It made him feel more fit.
He took to the forest with some soap, with
   A nickel's worth of nails and an axe —
Oh, how could he cope with
   Those early American fac's!
     He had a yen
     For Walden Glen —
The bushes and the rushes were his favorite den!
   Oh, Thoreau was a neuro!
   He liked Provincetown and Truro!
   Thoreau was a neuro, too!

He refused to pay his taxes
    And they put him in the cooler,
But he had his private axis —
    His undaunted animula.
He survived without commensals
    Where another man would break,
For he went on making pencils,
    Which he sharpened in the lake.

Oh, Thoreau was a neuro —
    Like us, I will repeat;
But it never made him pruro:
    His ideas remained sweet.
Tea was only tipple
    And he didn't know what hammocks were for;
But oh, how he loved to ripple the bosom of that
    water with an oar!
    He dipped his wand
    In Walden Pond —
He thought a sheet of water was a beautiful blonde!
    Oh, Thoreau was a neuro!
    A noble old cuckooro!
    Thoreau was a neuro, too!

ISADORE ELIZABETH FLANDERS
To Thoreau

They called you, Thoreau, hermit gray?
How could they know that on the day
The heifer came to snuff your hand,
Theocritus with all his band
          Piped joyfully?

How could they know, as lover, You?
With Autumn gay, a rendezvous!
Of how you kissed her burning lip,
Of how you lingered there to sip
          Sheer ecstasy.

How could they hear the silver bird
With flame tipped wing, you daily heard;
How could they see your hearth fires' glow
Tracing starblossom in the snow?
          You, hermit gray?

PAUL ENGLE
Henry David Thoreau

Keep your accounts, he urged, on your thumb nail,
Let your affairs be only two or three,
Accept, if days demand, the jealous jail
To prove the need of pure simplicity.
Suck all the marrow out of life and try
To dare the now as carefully as cattle
Enter the daily field, feel when you die
Your feet grow colder, hear your own throat rattle.

Whittle the wooden years with pocket knife,
Be free of heaven and in no man's bond,
Hold natural form, as a dog's tail its true
Curve, in desperate quiet lead your life,
A plain man dwelling proudly by a pond
Watching the sun down, moon down, earth down too.

HOWARD NUTT
Thoreau

I

New-rich New England, twittering and starched,
Still scratched herself in public, picked her nose,
And, on the sly, pursued the old bitch witch
With little moralmystic "ooes" and "ohs."

Because her ponds were deeper than her people,
New England was already half-past-God,
A wilderness of houses, barns, and steeples,
And right here, in this middle of the woods,

He sat down on the grass and felt the lump
Of evening in his throat.
A whirlpool of swallows over a hollow stump,
The shadows taking root,

Clean smell of water, earth odor and earth color,
And in his ear the near, thin whisper of blood,
(He and the cosmic woodchuck eyed each other)
—All this was episode,

Was incidental to the thought, the words
(That shocked New England like a growling gut
At Sunday morning worship), overheard
From Ireland to India—

                                    And yet,
The words were incidental to the man,
Who dared to live a long life all life long
Among these bricks and butterflies, among
New Englishmen, as humble as a stone.

II

Given the X of sex,
The economic facts,
The telescope approach
Case history, and such—
This little wink of a man
Remains phenomenon.

Disguised with wit, the hurt
Heart escapes our court.

Whatever gets an age
So vertical a one—
Horizon, heritage,
Or spots in the sun,
Too much, too little,
Head- heart- or belly-ache,
A gland gone wrong, the riddle
of self—whatever it takes
To make this sort of man,
Hallelujah! amen!

The practical man survives
A blizzard of butterflies.

III

Here was a man could tell you how much more
There is to poverty than being poor,
To greatness, than to be misunderstood—
But this would hardly make him great, or good:

It must have been the desperate innocence
With which he wrote bad verse and played a flute,
Kept to the woods, and made a State offense
Of how much he could get along without,

Took nothing for granted, spent his life
Keeping his ledger straight and his lip stiff,
While finding out about his final self
What a dog could tell at a whiff.

I don't know what you'd call this kind of man,
Doctor of Diddlers, Yankee Pan,
Prophet or prig, a glory or disgrace—
But people called him "Henry" to his face.

Inspirations Further into the Twentieth Century

But to the poet there are no riddles.
They are "pleasant songs" to him;
his faith solves the enigmas
which recurring wisdom does not fail to repeat.
—Journal, March 1841

WILLIAM BRONK
Flowers, the World and My Friend, Thoreau

It no longer matters what the names of flowers are.
Some I remember; others forget: ones
I never thought I should. Yes, tell me one.
I like to hear that. I may have forgotten again
next week. There's that yellow one whose name
I used to know. It's blossoming, secure
as ever as I walk by looking at it,
not saying its name or needing to.

Henry, it's true as you said it was, that this
is a world where there are flowers. Though it isn't our truth,
it's a truth we embrace with gratitude:
how should we endure our dourness otherwise?
And we feel an eager desire to make it ours,
making the flowers ours by naming them.

But they stay their own and it doesn't become our truth.

We live with it; live with othernesses
as strangers live together in crowds. Truths
of strangeness jostle me; I jostle them
walking past them as I do past clumps of flowers.
Flowers, I know you, not knowing your name.

MAXINE KUMIN
Beans

> ...*making the earth say beans instead of grass—*
> *this was my daily work.*
> —Thoreau, Walden

Having planted
that seven-mile plot
he came to love it
more than he had wanted.
His own sweat
sweetened it.
Standing pat
on his shadow
hoeing every noon
it came to pass
in a summer long gone
that Thoreau
made the earth say beans
instead of grass.

You, my gardener
setting foot
among the weeds
that stubbornly reroot
have raised me up
into hellos
expansive as
those everbearing rows.

Even without
the keepsake strings
to hold the shoots
of growing things
I know this much:
I say beans
at your touch.

ROBERT FRANCIS
Thoreau in Italy

Lingo of birds was easier than lingo of peasants—
they were elusive, though, the birds, for excellent reasons.
He thought of Virgil, Virgil who wasn't there to chat with.

History he never forgave for letting Latin
lapse into Italian, a renegade jabbering
musical enough but not enough to call music

So he conversed with stones, imperial and papal.
Even the preposterous popes he could condone
a moment for the clean arrogance of their inscriptions.

He asked the Italians only to leave him in the past
alone, but this was what they emphatically never did.
Being the present, they never ceased to celebrate it.

Something was always brushing him on the street, satyr
or saint—impossible to say which the more foreign.
At home he was called touchy; here he knew he was.

Impossible to say. The dazzling nude with sex
lovingly displayed like carven fruit, the black
robe sweeping a holy and unholy dust.

Always the flesh whether to lacerate or kiss—
conspiracy of fauns and clerics smiling back
and forth at each other acquiescently through leaves.

Caught between wan monastic mountains wearing the tonsure
and the all-siren, ever-dimpling sea, he saw
(how could he fail?) at heart geography to blame.

So home to Concord where (as he might have known he would)
he found the Italy he wanted to remember.
Why had he sailed if not for the savour of returning?

An Italy distilled of all extreme, conflict,
collusion—an Italy without the Italians—
in whose green context he could con again his Virgil.

In cedar he read cypress, in the wild apple, olive.
His hills would stand up favorably to the hills of Rome.
His arrowheads could hold their own with art Etruscan.

And Walden clearly was his Mediterranean
whose infinite colors were his picture gallery.
How far his little boat transported him—how far.

TOMAS TRANSTRÖMER
Five Stanzas to Thoreau

Yet another has left the heavy town's
ring of ravenous stones. Crystal and salty
is the water merging round the heads of all
true fugitives.

Here in a slow swirl silence has risen
from earth's midst, to take root and grow
and with bushy crown shadow the man's
sunwarm doorstep.

*

A foot carelessly kicks a mushroom. A thunder-
cloud swells on the horizon. Like copper horns
twisted treeroots sound and leaves
scatter in fright.

Autumn's headlong chase is his light cloak,
flapping until again from frost and ashes
calm days have come in flock to bathe their
claws in spring.

*

Disbelieved goes the one who has seen a geyser,
fled the stagnant well like Thoreau and knowing
thus to vanish deep in inner verdure,
cunning and hopeful.

DONALD JUNKINS
July

The clouds were fishbone
high. Downwind.
From the pond
watercolor rose toward the sun
like heat, and voices
carried from a boat.
Four feet from shore
two executive bass
meandered by,
bored by bait
and waiting.

    Armed,
a crawfish backed
from underneath a rock;
a boy amused his girl
by skipping stones
across the cove;
a lone Canada goose
dove under; some cloven crows
flapped out of a pine
like a frayed black bow
untying.

Summer had closed
in. At dusk
the waterfront began
to clear; tip-toeing
bathers crossed the gravel
to their cars. Kibbies
cupped their noses
up for flies and
popped the water-top. A band
of Negros with a banjo
settled in.

The smell
of warm fresh water
wafted toward the shore;
across the cove where
Thoreau built his
hut, seventy frogs
were bulling:
"chug-a-rum,
"chug-a-rum."
The night was opening
like a cotyledon.

MILTON KESSLER
The Good Death

For Henry David Thoreau a Century Later

O father of Concord, the war comes!
Beautiful blue children call in the eastern field.
Bird-songs? Wave after wave? And forever?
If the world could be like him and sing,
If I could build my naked fear into that ecstasy
As Henry once could do and sigh,
Or walk among the sad Waldens of the West
Where love evolves the sweet face
Of the seasons . . .. All men must lie.
Like inborn gentleness they find
Humiliation then art.
A real life? A pond of simple reasons?
The smile changing to taste the dark?
The deep lake within the ordinary woman you lost?

If Henry sang like this to sing,
All rising from his loneliness to spring,
Then no more excuses. The brave dream on.
The sleeping soldier smiles in the rain:
"A good death, a good death!"
It comes out of the future for me.

CHARLES TIDLER
Transcending the Sublime Henry David

A return to Nature
    isn't a Transcendental reading plan.
        Thoreau isn't

waiting up night for us,
    a bleeding amaranth in his hatband.
        His stick is walking ahead of his tune,

one stone at a stone's time.
    A creek of running hands
        moving in his lungs,

a song in his throat,
    maidens of mushrooms at his command.
        A cow path of soft cow shit,

branches hard with nipples,
    whippoorwills on a telegraph pole
        lasso sound before a rainstorm.

Clouds up to breathe.
    Moon in a dream,
        Thoreau walks the hills,

graphite and paper in his pocket,
    a phrase hooking itself up,
        a plow to a mare.

Dandelions everywhere.
    The stars pointing themselves out,
        a milky way in the making.

Thoreau knocks about the country,
    a frown in his jacket,
        a ball of yawn in his face,

Crickets in the sticks.
    Books on the table at home,
        open to a soft spot,

Milton or Browne,
    "the best parts of nothing,"
        ink points of emphasis in their margins.

But the handyman of Harvard
    has a date with a hook,
        crocuses of surprise in his eyes,

water in his brain.
    Thoreau lives in his boots,
        lives in his clothes.

He walks in his books
    the way he walks in a woods,
        or walks in a room.

The sound of an ax in a tree—
    a house goes up before you know,
        a window for the birds,

space to make some tea,
    honey and sugar
        in a sweet tooth time.

Thoreau is walking
    beneath the trees
        higher than him in Heaven.

BARRY TARGAN

Thoreau Stalks the Land Disguised as a Father

Thoreau stalks the land disguised as a father.
His bright children scurry before him
trampling gentians,
flushing neighborly grouse,
whacking trees with sticks
until all the animals flee
from the fierce tattoo.
But Thoreau, balding, breathless,
his coloring interior, bad,
marches to a different drumbeat.

His lamed wife hobbles after him,
calling him to wait,
to walk slower,
to help carry the enormous bundle
they live from.
But Thoreau is looking for paths,
trails, old footfalls. A way.
Thoreau is lost in the forest.
He remembers nothing of this
fury of conifers and beech.

All he remembers is a languid pond.
He looks for the pond to guide him,
to follow the pond home

as once he followed Polaris.
There! Behind the thick stand of hemlock!
The pond!
But the pond is deep in his head.
He stumbles into a ditch,
a ravine carved by the March
run-off of melting snow.

The sons howl like wolves.
The wife catches up.
He has ripped the patch on his knee
and the skin beneath it.

Tonight they will camp here.

HAI ZI (ZHA HAISHENG)
Thoreau Has Brains

1
This guy, Thoreau, has got brains
Like fish have water, birds have wings
Clouds have the sky

2.
Fortunately, he was not a woman
Else there would be a pair
Of white polar bears
On the road, staggering
Clinging to his breasts
Their lips approaching

3.
Thoreau has brains
Thoreau has nothing else at hand
He grabs a stick
That stick hits me
Hits me hard, as Spring has hit me

4.
Thoreau has brains
Happy whenever he sees the pond

5.
Thoreau has brains
He made a postbox out of a bird nest
Two letters arrive at the same time
Then give birth to many short letters
Feathers a-floating

6.
Thoreau has brains
In silence, he ushers in dawn from the east window
lets darkness reign the west window
But when does he have a window?

Thoreau has brains
In silence, he is both a man, and a woman
In fact, the son he begets is still himself

7.
A cabin with lights on
Lies Thoreau's Helmet
—A volume of Homer

Thoreau has brains
He turns snow into a horse
Leading me across the water

8.
Thoreau has brains
Moonlight shines on his nose

9.
That lyrical nose
Close to his mind
Close to his eyes as deep as the woods
Close to his lips drinking the water
(May he drink more deeply)

Form the skull
Or the head

10.
Day and night
Like black and white
Two docile cats
napping on your shoulders

You fall on the road in the forest

Let the bed lie sick in the cabin
Thoreau has brains
Makes wildflowers bear fruit

11.
This guy, Thoreau, has got brains
Like fish have water, birds have wings
Clouds have the sky

This person Thoreau
My cloud, cloud from all land
around me, quiet
To the west of the Bean Field
On my straw hat

12.
The sun, The beans
I planted, offering my lips
I let the water gush down the river

Thoreau has brains
Thoreau's Helmet
—A volume of Homer

PARKMAN HOWE
Letter from Wachusett

> *But special I remember thee,*
> *Wachusett, who like me*
> *Standest alone without society.*
>   Henry David Thoreau, A Walk to Wachusett

Dear Henry,

You made your walk west, "at a cool
and early hour," mid-July, 1842,
with Richard Fuller, Margaret's younger brother.

You tramped the dust track through the woods
of Acton and Stowe, west to Wachusett,
the Great Hill, 25 miles. At noon
you took your ease on a ridge in Lancaster,
reading Virgil, thinking of Rome and
the south of France; you descended to
the Nashua River; in the unstirring
air of afternoon you sauntered into
the forest, observing dogsbane
and pokeberry beside a leafy brook.

Four miles from Wachusett, on the banks
of the Stillwater, you halted for the night;
in your room at the inn you overheard
"the murmuring of water… the slumberous
breathing of crickets."

                  We make our outing
from the subdivisions of Concord,
a family of three, mid-July, 1990.
We drive Route 2 west to 140 south,
burning fossil fuels, sixty miles an hour;
we reach Wachusett in 30 minutes;
on the radio, news of the Antarctic,
the melting airbank shield of ozone.

In the lead light of dawn you clambered through
a sugar bush, then dense, dwarf hemlock
to the summit, the two of you alone.

At the landscaped visitor center we
park, hike the blazed trail, map in hand.

In the open summit acres you found
blueberries, raspberries, goose- and strawberries,
moss, and a fine, wiry grass; yellow
lily and dwarf cornel flourished in
crevices of rock; you noted robins,
swallows; you got wind of chewinks, cuckoos.

At the highest point, you wrote, a wooden
observatory had given way to
its stone foundation; the firmament so
hazy, Monadnock, blue in the far north-
west, seemed a Pacific island of ether.

On the summit today: an Army Corps
building, a memorial to the 10th
Mountain Division, a fire tower
fenced off by barbed wire. Half a dozen
families picnic on exposed granite
tufted with grass and mud; paired with their cars
they are etched against airy horizon;
sparrows squabble over bread crumbs among
crumbling concrete foundations.

                                       In your
tent you read Virgil, Wordsworth; you dined on
milk and blueberries, for evensong
the thrush, her sharp, flute-like *pit pit pit pit*.
That night the nearly full moon so bright
you read "distinctly by moonlight." A fire
on Monadnock lit the whole northwest
prospect; at home among the community
of mountains you felt less solitary;
at times you woke to wind roaring over rocks.

For us, Monadnock in the northwest haze
"in simple grandeur," as you perceived;
to the south the needle spires of Worcester,
farther eastward the half-dozen towers
of Boston like blue pencil erasers.

You witnessed the transparent atmosphere,
the cold, windless sunrise; then kindled
a fire that might be descried thirty miles.

Fifty years after your climb a road
was cut to the summit, a summit
hotel constructed; replaced three times,
the last built in 1907; closed
during World War II; in 1970
it burned to the ground.

                    Now the reservation
advertises 17 miles of hiking
and snowshoeing trails, eleven miles of
cross-country ski trails, 103 acres
of downhill skiing, with lodge and base
facilities; sometimes, in spring azalea
season, or fall foliage, 10,000
visitors drive to Wachusett on a
single day.

                At noon you decamped; by nightfall
you reached the town of Harvard; the next day
Fuller proceeded to Groton; you tramped
your singular path "to the peaceful
meadows of Concord." "On this side the valley
of Merrimack," you later wrote, "on that
of the Connecticut, fluctuating
with their blue seas of air — these rival vales,
already teaming with Yankee men along
their respective streams, born to what destiny
who shall tell?"

		Loss accelerates: war, fire,
neglect, greed; we are an agitated,
impatient people. Even here, deep in
the woods, alone on the homeward trail,
the leaves hushed and cooling overhead,
our boots scuff the mountain gravel loose.

JOHN ENRIGHT
Teaching Thoreau

There was a horse in the graveyard today.
The same graveyard that was a lake
with stonetops for whitecaps two weeks ago
when it rained.
        Today it is clear, the brown horse
is tethered, all ribs on sticks, and wanders
distractedly down a grass aisle.

I taught Thoreau today and nobody got it
and I had to carry it all back with me
through the green sun of the campus,
                              wondering
where I had gone wrong.
The graveyard is on the way home.
I pass it twice a day,
    sometimes in flood, sometimes in famine.

BARRY STERNLIEB
Thoreau's Hat

1.

On a long afternoon walk
pockets run out of room:
stones, acorns, wild fruit,
an arrowhead, a bone.
There must be someplace safe
for one fringed gentian,
half a black swallowtail,
or an owlfeather
still holding the moon!

2.

Five miles to go
until dusk fills the pond,
but there's no hurry.
Nothing comes between this mind
and the world it is
collecting, whose smallest details
are worth looking into
for what they make of us.

3.

Back home, with the harvest
lined up on the table,
he checks each object closely
and writes a few words down
while a hornet walks the brim
of his faded hat
completely unnoticed,
around and around as if
we might never be born.

TIMOTHY LIU
Thoreau

My father and I have no place to go.
His wife will not let us in the house—
afraid of catching AIDS. She thinks
sleeping with men is more than a sin,
my father says, as we sit on the curb
in front of someone else's house.
Sixty-four years have made my father
impotent. Silver roots, faded black
dye mottling his hair make him look
almost comical, as if his shame
belonged to me. Last night we read
Thoreau in a steakhouse down the road
and wept: *If a man does not keep pace
with his companions, let him travel
to the music that he hears, however
measured or far away.* The orchards
are gone, his village near Shanghai
bombed by the Japanese, the groves
I have known in Almaden—apricot,
walnut, peach and plum—hacked down.

EDWARD MORIN

Labor Day at Walden Pond

> *for Jim Nani*
> "...they know whether they are well employed..."
> –H. D. Thoreau

Both narrow shoulders of Rte. #126
(marked "No Standing" for 3/4 of a mile
past the Pond to the Concord town limit)
are jammed with cars single-file, parking free.
The $4-buck lot in front stands almost empty.

Citizens with the law in their own hands
mill through big pines on Walden Reservation.
The master's words fly on the cool west wind:
Where there is a lull of truth, up springs the
state's Department of Natural Resources.

Bathhouse, johns, lifeguard, lots of sunbathers
crowd the east end. The far shore still looks fresh.
Waves peak and sparkle in late afternoon.
One frog is croaking to a different drummer:
you have to call this much water a lake.

A path along the northern shore—the deep side—
leads past a cove to a bare clearing where
Thoreau lived a year in a shack that cost
$62.00, including food and clothes.
No clouds today. No boards left on the site.

A small crowd watches where the great man worked
more trades than he had toes or fingers. Profit,
like the railroad, still rides us. Men with jobs
run out of work. We disband toward wherever
we must—a shrinking week. Summer is over.

Third Century Voices

The wisest definition of poetry the poet will instantly prove false by setting aside its requisitions.
—A Week on the Concord and Merrimack Rivers

MARY OLIVER
Going to Walden

It isn't very far as highways lie.
I might be back by nightfall, having seen
The rough pines, and the stones, and the clear water.
Friends argue that I might be wiser for it.
They do not hear that far-off Yankee whisper:
How dull we grow from hurrying here and there!

Many have gone, and think me half a fool
To miss a day away in the cool country.
Maybe. But in a book I read and cherish,
Going to Walden is not so easy a thing
As a green visit. It is the slow and difficult
Trick of living, and finding it where you are.

AARON SILVERBERG
Thoreau's Chair

Chocolate-brown maple and slightly askew
it sits empty
or so it seems
to the casual viewer.

Only one today,
on others
there are two for friendship or
three for society.

A peculiar light provides
patient reflection of what's there.

This is where the creator sits,
resting amid the songs and stories
of common folk.

Henry David came upon the wood
to confront what persisted
to befriend what subsisted.

I reserve his chair for you, beloved reader,
perpetual gift to the Guest that visits,
that wanders monkishly bemused.

Sit a spell in it, bedazzled.

CHARLIE MEHRHOFF
Spring Birdlife

I should go stand
in the entrance
of the new super Walmart
and tear out pages of WALDEN—
just hand them out
to all who enter.
Probably, I'd get busted
for being a terrorist—
worse stuff than Anthrax
this notion that freedom
just might be possible.

J. WALTER BRAIN
The Loon at Walden

Stranded, apart, or adventure bent,
The loon rides the margins of ponds
As ice tightens a noose and entraps
Water, wood, feather, and fat.
The bird takes off into the air
Bound for another pond at winter's
Edge. Thus stops the loon at Walden
To snoop its depths and snatch a meal
Before ice closes in again.
He plays the game, with peals of laughter
At nature's never ending siege.
There he emerges, fresh from the deep,
A bulky bird, stout of bill,
Serene in poise and self-possessed,
To ride the ripples in stately drift
And a loon's mind to stay the course—
Alone, alert, or lame, defying
Death, to seize the hour and revel
In every morsel snatched from the teeth
Of Mors himself, by the ice's edge.

INGELA STRANDBERG
Dear Mr. Thoreau!

Dear Mr. Thoreau, the owls
have been here again. Do not speak ill
of the owls' song. They just wish to warn
me. They say that my
loneliness is threatened and that soon I will no longer
be able to walk out on the road without meeting someone.
The landscape is a poisoned rat
which retreats to die
when I try to help it.

The birds, Mr. Thoreau,
rest with the dead.

DAVID STARKEY

Allen Ginsberg in Thoreau's Maine Woods

Cold, soaking, wrapped in wet wool, I lean
      towards sputtering camp fire,
            tin mug of coffee
in chapped red hands, burrs in socks,
      runny nose, Heaven clapped
to forehead. Buddha-memories, Blake painting,
      stoned on wildflowers in thick pine forest—
Skullcap, Meadow-Rue, St. John's Wort,
          Black Snake-
Root, Common Virgin's Bower.

          No virgin, I
mind-breathe native hymns, Om Ah Hum.
          Nasal strain of our guide,
      Savage nobler than any Captain Amerika—
shrewd chants, not trivial Republocrat
      Wall Street Journal radio exchange songs,
            but Tremors, War, Sadness
& Love Lost on banks of black northern rivers—
      Umbazookskus, Chesuncook, Caucomgomoc.

Comely Animals howl, mad promenade in Bohemian
       Ktaadn night. Lynx, Sable, Hedgehog,
            Beaver, Otter, Moose
gulp lungfuls of Alder scent, sweet Choke-Cherry
             & Mountain Holly,
furious fur tossed towards bitch-goddess Diana—
        myriad paws waving at white orb, sole
     solace in this wretched, lovely, pitch-blind,
         viscous wilderness of screams.

JOHN KINSELLA

Sacred Kingfisher and Trough Filled with Water Pumped from Deep Underground

> *It is the work of art nearest to life itself.*
> —Thoreau, Walden, 'Reading'

With the record heat I filled one of the three
concrete troughs — mainly for kangaroos
but also for birds and anything else that passes
by. This morning I saw a sacred kingfisher
in an overhanging branch, eyeing the water.
The sacred kingfisher saw me and remained.
That's unusual — they are mostly cautious.
I over-invest the 'sacred' in their name — name
giving, name evoking statistics from those
who've probably not even seen the bird. A small
bird with a large beak that could inflict a lot
of damage on whatever it targets. Proportional
and relative. Its colours are flashy and stunning.
What part do I play in filling the trough, once
for sheep and horses? How much choice
to come and go does the sacred kingfisher
have? Would it be here if the trough was empty?
The valley was quiet in the broadest sense.
I did not know how much noise was within

the bird's head. I thought of Thoreau
thinking of Alexander the Great carrying
the *Iliad* in a special casket. Which now
makes me think of a coffin. Water-troughs
look like coffins, like caskets. I expected
the sacred kingfisher to swoop as if the shallow
water held nourishment. It was dead water
from deep in the earth. The sacred kingfisher
stayed in the branch, seeing the trough
for the coffin it was. The bird looked at me
then looked back to the lifeless surface
of the water. Still . . . so still.

IAN MARSHALL
Higher Laws

an impulse to eat woodchuck
   not for my hunger
      but for his wildness

seeking venison
   loving the wild
      not less than the good

into the forest
   a hunter at first
      then leaving the gun behind

fishing
   sediment
      sinking to the bottom

a hook of hooks
   angling
      for the pond itself

fishing less and less
   a faint intimation
      the first streaks of morning

harvest of daily life
    the tint of morning and
        a little star-dust caught

inspired through the palate
    berries
        eaten on a hillside

jawbone of a hog
    sound teeth and tusks
        a creature that succeeded

a cool evening
    the sound of a flute
        stars over far fields

DAVID WAGONER
Thoreau and the Lightning

The white ash tree, the one he'd visited
        time after time and season after season
and had studied and admired like a proud father,
        had been struck by lightning. Lightning
had gouged downward, tossing broken limbs
        every which way, had split the trunk
into six twenty-foot, splayed, upstanding fence rails
        still held up by the roots, had ploughed a furrow
into a cellar (where it scorched the milk pans),
        had bolted out in a shower of soil, had shattered
weatherboards and beams and the foundation,
        had smashed a shed, unstacked and scattered a woodpile,
had flung pieces of bark two hundred feet
        in all directions. It had thrown into disorder
or destroyed in a moment what an honest farmer
        had struggled for years to gather, and had killed
a great tree. Was he supposed to be humbled
        by the benign, malign, inscrutable purposes
of the Source, the blundering Maker of Thunderheads,
        and be glad he hadn't been standing under it?

L.M. BROWNING
On the Far Side of Walden

Ankle-deep in mud
along the banks of Walden,
I find my footing.

Standing in the ruins of the cabin,
I return home to meet the brother
born before my time.

We souls close in ideals
but distant in years
keep council together.

When one of us passes along
the next will pick up the thread
and carry on the thought.

Walking the rim of Walden
the wheel of my life takes a turn.

The waters are a mirror
and the banks a respite.

On the far side of Walden
one can look out across the wide waters
and see the world reflecting.

It is a place in the journey
where one can take solace,
pause and look back with clear perspective.

Coming to the end of the path
I am not who I was
at the beginning.

CAMMY THOMAS
Refraction

I go to Walden Pond to convert my solitude.
It's dinnertime, sun low to the water, trees
in alpenglow. Believing there are no sharks,
I let my legs dangle. On my back, slightly submerged,
I watch the sun through a few inches of clear water,
 as it wobbles and spreads its warm diffused rays—
spears of light, flexing saddles of it. Each bubble
reflects the light, vibrating above my face.
I'm floating in the refractions of the sky.

Nothing comes to me.
No giant creature opens its jaws on my back.
I'm in the water, every cell cooling,
my mind on fire with beauty. It's not a musical—
no children show up to sing about how happy we are,
and the wise old people don't dance on shore to
welcome me home. But cradled by the water I feel the beast retreat.
Yes, I am alone, and no, that show of light
 and color is not for me—it merely exists in implacable nature.
Right now I can float in it.

TODD DAVIS

Thoreau Casts a Line in the Merrimack

Pickerel, pout, eel, salmon, shad, even more
fish than these swim in the waters of the Self

where he casts again, hoping to catch, to feed,
to release some back into the river's current,

which runs from west to east, the watercourse
of our making, our perishing, mortal bodies:

the milling wheel that carries us over the bones
of the earth and allows us to flow outward

beneath the stars and the heavens, the other
rivers running through the glistening black.

SUSAN BLACKWELL RAMSEY
How to Seduce Henry David Thoreau

It would help if you could be a loon
or, more ethereal, the evening star
or the sound of a wooden flute at sunset.
Otherwise, it's going to take all summer.

Be more ethereal than the evening star
to begin with, then start coming closer,
otherwise, it's going to take all summer.
Practice learning to walk like a doe.

Begin distant, then start coming closer
at evening, down there by the water's edge.
(Practice learning to walk like a doe.)
Don't look at him. Pretend he isn't there.

At evening, down there by the water's edge,
wearing your hair long and dressed in white,
not looking up, as if he weren't there,
remember that you mustn't say a word.

Of course your hair is long and you wear white.
Remember, he knows no girls, only maidens.
Silence helps him seduce himself.
Celibates are irresistible.

Even knowing no girls, only maidens,
his high principles are still wrapped in flesh.
If you find celibates irresistible,
over a whole summer you might win.

His high principles are wrapped in flesh
and mystery might win, but ask yourself
why you find celibates irresistible.
I'm not that interested, but you should be.

Mystery might win, but ask yourself
why it would help if you could be a loon.
I'm not that interested, but you should be
the sound of a wooden flute at sunset.

GENE G. BRADBURY
Lament

> *No other creature effects such changes in nature as man.*
> Thoreau's Journal Entry for November 3, 1853

It's gone now, like a quarter
in a magician's handkerchief,
demolished like T.E. Scott's* house
by order of the Town Council.

Lost like the keys searched for,
not where they're supposed to be.
The young boy's picture changed
into an old man's photograph.

Where is the track of pasture,
woodland orchard and swamp,
marked by the Carlisle Road,
when Henry saw blue laurel buds?

Does Thoreau still wander there,
standing in Mason's Pasture,
smelling pitch pine
as he did long ago?

*Early pioneer of Tescott, Kansas

CECILY PARKS
When I was Thoreau at Night

I covered my head so as to better hide
from men and see the moon, with whom
I carried on a conversation that illuminated

like lantern-swing, iterating and reiterating trees.
I asked, *What is my wild original?*
The moon said, *You dream me.*

Underfoot, aromatic crush.
I said, *I marry you.* The moon said, *You cannot husband me.*
Overhead, darkness circuited through

its diamond guides. If I were lonely, I loved loneliness.
If I were hungry, I ate battered apples. One star said, *Pilgrim.*
One star said, *Peregrine.* Peregrine. The name

of the first English child born in the brackish
New World. How I envied him, crying into
the wilderness with a name meaning wanderer.

My name seemed tame. How I hoped the farmers
would not find me in this woods, wearing this dress.
I asked the stars, *Will you be my jewelry?*

The stars said, *Follow us.* They drew me deep
into the disheveled spruces to introduce me
to loss. My fields were ill. They weren't my fields.

My trees were being killed. They weren't my trees.
I was nervous that this natural world would see
that I was filthy-footed in silk, a woman

pretending to be the man
to trip a pyrotechnic grace. Oh yes,
I wanted the world to be wild again. I believed

I might hold weather in my hands
and mend it. The night was finite, or infinite.
Expending my expiring decadence in modern

thirst, I tempted biography to invent me.
Weird nun in the night garden, I dipped my face,
yes, my face, in every honeyed pond and could not drink.

CORINNE HOSFELD SMITH

Notes on Thoreau's Notes from Mackinac Island
Reactions to excerpts from his 1861 trip field notebook

"Arbor vitae about sides of island;"
Henry observed, and then quickly penned.
He and friend Horace botanized
And made species lists that they scrutinized.
Mackinac was an interesting place
That they could study at their own pace.
They'd probably never seen cedars this tall
With trunks as thick as maples and all.

"Apple in bloom … & lilac."
Thoreau was surprised, because way back
In Concord, both trees blossomed in May.
But this far north, Nature's clock is delayed.
And now on these summery days of late June,
He could shockingly still inhale lilac perfume.
His hometown phenology couldn't help here
To predict or explain when flowers appeared.

"Spring disappears in stones of shore."
At Dwightwood Spring, did Henry pour
Himself a cup of limestone dew
That burst up near the Arch Rock view?
And did he turn to catch the sun
Emerging from beyond Huron?
Did passing freighters break his gaze
Amidst the flare of morning's rays?

"Sat by fire July 2d."
Did his consumption suddenly beckon?
Had he exhausted himself that much
After three days of constant walking and such?
Or was the air so brisk at night
That it required a beach camp site?
I'd like to think the evenings were cold
And that his illness was somewhat controlled.

His notes are short. He never took
The time to create a new travelogue book.
Consumption came back, off and on,
And by mid-May, Henry was gone.
He left us pages of scribbled notes,
And we can follow the clues he wrote.
We retrace paths that he had known
Until the adventure becomes our own.

AMY NAWROCKI
The Charity Houses of Cape Cod

This is what Thoreau
called those rickety
and shingled bungalows

that braced the wind-swept
dune sands with the kind
of poise given to

the most humble
of structures, when
wooden planks know

they are no match
for the tyranny
and heartlessness

of sea storms. When
he walked along
the Cape Cod shoreline,

Thoreau's mapmaker feet
followed the path
his mind sought between

the Nauset Plains
and Highland Light,
the urge to become

a little more salted
seeping into his skin.
In these small shacks

he found company,
even when no other souls
were about—comfort

from a lonely stretch
of steady, barren beach.
Shelter, whatever

form it takes—whether
the lucky shade
of the high cumulus,

or the calm, temporary
sedation of low tide,
or even a sloped roof

suspended with the architecture
of nails and grooved logs
over a dry, simple place—shelter

gives respite of the sort
that clams know
pausing in the sand

before the gulls
with their appetite and spite
return to feed.

GINNY LOWE CONNORS
Thoreau's Pumpkins

It is thought that Henry David Thoreau was the first American to plant Potiron Jaune Grosse, a variety of large yellow pumpkin.

Six seeds from France began it all.
    No abracadabra required, no alacazam—
    just a bit of manure, some hoeing
    a little rain, and patience.

Where never they were seen before
    my giant pumpkins grow.
    Thick, prickly vines, green glossy leaves—and look!
    Over 100 pounds this one is, a marvel, a golden throne!

Seated upon it, content is what I am
    in the lovely light of clear bright days
    meadowlarks for company
    clouds floating by—angels in billowing skirts.

Farmers at Middlesex Fair gaze in awe
    as a juggler draws ribbons from his throat,
    though it's all deception. What amazes me
    is how the earth blazes with sunflowers and sun fruits.

Townswomen shut themselves in cushioned rooms
        thick with malarial air.
        They hold hands in the dark
        hoping to hear from the dead.

As for me, I look out at the pond
        listen to the gossip of bees, tend my garden.
        I have great faith in a seed—
        it prepares me to expect wonders.

Note: Some phrases come from Thoreau's manuscript, "Wild Fruits."

ALISON CROGGON

Sonnet: Thoreau in Chernobyl

The woods were beautiful as always, but dry.
It seemed a subtle poison at the roots
drained them imperceptibly of life.
A want, or heightened colour, in each leaf
hinted profound disease, as if the rites
of generation faltered and withdrew
beyond emergencies of flood and fire
to deserts that no green could penetrate.
I shaped my stanzas, but the form seemed trite:
all metre euphemised a deepening flaw.
I heard no frog calls, and the birds were fewer
in species and in number. I trod
ungodly glows, a covenant betrayed,
a humus rotting slowly into fear.

DAVID K. LEFF
Vain Strivings Untied

> *Be it life or death, we crave only reality.*
> –H. D. Thoreau

With faith in seeds
you bravely sowed furrows of words
for a harvest you'd never see.

Now comes a crop of long overdue
letters from that distant land
of ever receding futures.

Little solitude prevails at Walden,
full of summer swimmers
and visitors on well worn paths.

Staring into earth's deep eye,
pilgrims pine for answers
where you sunk fathomless questions.

I'm one of many dowsers turning
your pages like divining rods, probing
veins of truth veiled by rising vapors.

Simplicity seems complicated
among spinning motors, tract houses,
strip malls and electric amplification.

You could easily put your foot through
this contorted world where news
is faked, phones smart, and reality virtual.

But, your voice still whispers in snowstorms,
sounds in tumbling streams,
screams with the silence of stones.

I listen carefully, chancing upon
disparate moments of quiet inspiration
to cast a line on my own nearby pond.

JANICE MILLER POTTER
Thoreau's Umbrella

Rain, a cherishing.
From time to time slate
holds its burst.

Time and again, relents,
letting cold April
pour through the woods.

Tensed, then loosening,
drops break
clean from cloud.

The pond's slick slope
eases, paths
wrinkle into rivulets.

The first spring rain
loiters upon
a seine of trees.

He loves this place,
flow drumming
every cell.

Thut! Thut! Thut!
Myriads upon
myriads—the Real—

In the womb of spring,
he inhales its wet
scent on his umbrella.

JOHN REIBETANZ
Thoreau's Pencils

All change is a miracle to contemplate he writes
contemplating the pond's daily miracles how ice
forms in winter first printing the surface with crystal

leaves as if it flowed into moulds pressed on the liquid
mirror by the veined hands of waterplants and he writes
of bubbles clear bubbles honeycombing surface ice

in spring sun turning each to a burning-glass that melts
thick shards beneath or dark bubbles of frogspawn sprouting
tails and light-catching eyes he writes in pencil because

making pencils is the family livelihood and
because bubbles of ink dry unchangeable staining
the paper's fibres into mourning while the oar-strokes

of a pencil leave no trace on the freshened surface
when wind-smoothed by an eraser's sweeps and where pens seek
the icy might of swords the pencil takes a meek course

yielding line by line every sharpened point a whittling
down yet every glossy-barked cedar shaft liveliest
at its core the graphite that can carry thought from mind

through hand to paper a heartwood most unbreakable
he discovers when mixed as we are with clay *Am I*
he writes *not partly leaves and vegetable mould myself?*

NOTES ON CONTRIBUTORS

A. Bronson Alcott was an educator, transcendentalist philosopher, writer, social reformer, and friend of Thoreau. His pedagogical approach favored a conversational style, abjured corporeal punishment, and explored new ways of reaching younger students.

Louisa May Alcott is best known for her world famous novel *Little Women* (1868), but also published over a dozen books, including novels and short stories. Thoreau was one of her early teachers. Other volumes in the *Little Women* trilogy are *Little Men: Life at Plumfield with Jo's Boys* (1871), and *Jo's Boys and How They Turned Out: A Sequel to "Little Men"* (1886).

Gene G. Bradbury writes from the Pacific Northwest where he lives with his wife, Debbie. Among his 10,000-book library are many by and about Henry David Thoreau. His book of poetry entitled: *Sauntering With Thoreau* (2014) is among his publications of twenty-two books.

J. Walter Brain was a landscape architect and active member of the Thoreau Society. His poems frequently appeared in the Society's quarterly *Thoreau Society Bulletin* as well as in the annual, *The Concord Saunterer*.

William Bronk won the National Book Award in 1982 for his poetry collection *Life Supports*. Among his over 30 books of poetry are: *Light and Dark* (1956), *That Beauty Still* (1978), *Some Words* (1992), and *Metaphor of Trees and Last Poems* (1999).

(L.M.) Leslie M. Browning is a TEDx talker, photojournalist, and the award-winning author of twelve titles. In her writing, Browning explores the confluence of the natural landscape and the interior landscape. She has served on the board of the Independent Book Publishers Association and is a fellow with the International League of Conservation Writers. In 2011, she founded Homebound Publications and its divisions, now a leading independent publisher.

William Ellery Channing frequently took walks with his friend Henry David Thoreau. He was a transcendentalist poet and wrote the first Thoreau biography: *Thoreau: The Poet-Naturalist (1873)*. His other books include: *Poems, Second Series* (1847), *The Woodsman* (1849), and *John Brown and the Heroes of Harper's Ferry* (1886).

Ginny Lowe Connors is the author of several poetry collections, including *Toward the Hanging Tree: Poems of Salem Village* (2016). Her chapbook, *Under the Porch* (2010), won the Sunken Garden Poetry Prize, and she has earned numerous awards for individual poems. As publisher of her own press, Grayson Books, Connors has also edited a number of poetry anthologies, including *Forgotten Women: A Tribute in Poetry* (2017). She is co-editor of *Connecticut River Review*.

Alison Croggon is an award winning and widely published Australian poet, playwright, opera librettist, and novelist. Her poetry books include *Attempts at Being* (2002), *The Common Flesh: New and Selected Poems* (2003), *November Burning* (2004), and *Ash* (2007).

Todd Davis is a former fellow of the Black Earth Institute and the author of six collections of poetry, most recently *Native Species* (2019) and *Winterkill* (2016). His writing has won the Foreword INDIES Book of the Year Bronze and Silver Awards, the Gwendolyn Brooks Poetry Prize, the Chautauqua Editors Prize, and the Bloomsburg University Book Prize. He teaches environmental studies, American literature, and creative writing at Pennsylvania State University's Altoona College.

Ralph Waldo Emerson was a poet, essayist, and leading transcendentalist philosopher who started his career as a Unitarian minister in Boston. He was mentor and friend of Henry David Thoreau. Emerson achieved world renown as a lecturer and author of such essays as "Self-Reliance," "History," "The Over-Soul," and "Fate."

Paul Engle Spent many years as director of the Iowa Writer's Workshop. He was a poet, editor, teacher, literary critic, novelist, and playwright. Among his many poetry collections are *Worn Earth* (1932), *West of Midnight* (1941), and *Poems in Praise* (1959).

John Enright wrote "Teaching Thoreau" while teaching at American Samoa Community College. His collection of poems from Samoa, *14 Degrees South* (2012), won the University of the South Pacific Press's inaugural International Literature Competition.

Isadore Elizabeth Flanders was a teacher in Saginaw, Michigan. Her books include *The Red Upon The Hill* (1930), *By Chance* (1931), and *A Thimble Cup* (1939).

Robert Francis wrote more than half a dozen volumes of poetry, and was praised by his mentor Robert Frost. His second collection *Valhalla and Other Poems* (1938) won the Shelley Memorial Award in 1939. In 1984, the Academy of American Poets gave Francis its award for distinguished poetic achievement. *Collected Poems 1936-1976* came out in 1976.

Parkman Howe edits poetry for *Appalachia: America's Longest-Running Journal of Mountaineering and Conservation*. He is a retired teacher living in Carlisle, Massachusetts, where he keeps bees.

Donald Junkins was the author of eleven books of poetry and two novels. He directed the MFA Program at University of Massachusetts, Amherst, for ten years, where he taught for three decades. Among his books of poetry are *The Sunfish and the Partridge* (1965), *Walden:100 Years After Thoreau* (1968), *Late at Night in the Rowboat* (2005), and *Burning the Leaves* (2018).

Milton Kessler wrote six books of poetry, was an English professor at Binghamton University, and a founder of the university's creative writing program. Among his books are *A Road Came Once*, (1963), *The Grand Concourse*, (1990), and the posthumous *Free Concert: New and Selected Poems*, (2002).

John Kinsella is an Australian poet. His most recent poetry volumes include *Jam Tree Gully* (2012), *Drowning in Wheat: Selected Poems* (2016), and *Insomnia* (2019). He has also written fiction, criticism, and plays, and often works in collaboration with other writers, artists and musicians. He is a Fellow of Churchill College, Cambridge, and professor of literature and environment, Curtin University, Western Australia.

Florence Kiper Frank is best known for her poetry collection, *The Jew to Jesus and Other Poems* (1915). She published poems widely in *Poetry* and other literary journals, and also wrote plays and children's books. *The Silver Grain* (1956) is another poetry collection.

Maxine Kumin wrote eighteen poetry collections as well as numerous novels, essays, memoirs, and children's books. She won the Pulitzer Prize for Poetry in 1973 for *Up Country* (1972). From 1981–1982, she served as the poetry consultant to the Library of Congress (now called U.S. Poet Laureate).

David K. Leff is the author of six nonfiction books, three volumes of poetry, and two novels in verse. He is poet laureate of Canton, Connecticut. By appointment of the National Park Service he served as poet-in-residence for the New England National Scenic Trail (NET) for 2016-17.

Timothy Liu is the author of twelve books of poems, most recently *Let It Ride* (2019). He is a reader of occult esoterica.

James Russell Lowell was a powerful literary critic, poet, Harvard professor, magazine editor, essayist, and diplomat. His books include *The Biglow Papers* (1848) *A Fable for Critics* (1848), *Among My Books* (1870), and *My Study Windows* (1871).

Ian Marshall is a professor of English and environmental studies at Penn State Altoona and a former president of the Association for the Study of Literature and Environment. Among his books are: *Story Line: Exploring the Literature of the Appalachian Trail* (1998), *Peak Experiences: Walking Meditations on Literature, Nature, and Need* (2003), *Walden by Haiku* (2009), and *Border Crossings: Walking the Haiku Path on the International Appalachian Trail*.

Charlie Mehrhoff, a former desert dweller, attempts to live as quietly as possible in the North Woods. His books of poetry are *Words to Light Eternity* (2020) and *We Have Come to Believe* (2020). One of his children's books, *A Wrecking Ball for Angel*, was recently published.

Edward Morin's poems have appeared in *Hudson Review, Ploughshares,* and *Prairie Schooner*. Collections of his poetry include *The Dust of Our City* (1978), *Labor Day at Walden Pond* (1997), and *Housing for Wrens* (2016). He edited, and with Dennis Ding and Dai Fang co-translated, *The Red Azalea: Chinese Poetry since the Cultural Revolution* (1990). He co-hosts the Crazy Wisdom Poetry Series of readings and writers' workshops in Ann Arbor.

Amy Nawrocki is the author of six poetry collections, most recently *Mouthbrooders* (2019), a finalist for the Connecticut Book Award. *The Comet's Tail: A Memoir of No Memory* (2018) was a 2018 Foreword Review INDIES finalist for best memoir and has been awarded a Mind Award from Living Now Books. She teaches literature and creative writing and lives in Hamden Connecticut.

Mary Oliver's many books of poetry include *No Voyage, and Other Poems* (1963), *Blue Horses* (2014), *West Wind* (1997), *Red Bird* (2008), and *A Thousand Mornings* (2012). Her collections have won the National Book Award and the Pulitzer Prize.

Howard Nutt was an African-American poet and leftist organizer who published in *Poetry, The New Republic,* and *The Yale Review*. His best-known book is *Special Laughter* (1940), which featured an introduction by Richard Wright.

Cecily Parks is the author of the poetry collections *Field Folly Snow* (2008) *and O'Nights* (2015). She is the editor of *The Echoing Green: Poems of Fields, Meadows, and Grasses* (2016). She teaches at Texas State University. Her work has appeared in *The New Yorker, Kenyon Review, Orion*, and *The Yale Review*.

Janice Miller Potter is the author of three poetry collections: *Thoreau's Umbrella* (2019), *Meanwell* (2012), and *Psalms in Time* (2008). Her poems have also appeared in various journals and anthologies, including *Poet Lore, Bloodroot, The Fourth River, and Connecticut Review*. She lives in Cornwall, Vermont.

Susan Blackwell Ramsey is the author of *A Mind Like This* (2012), which won the Prairie Schooner Book Prize in Poetry. She lives in Kalamazoo, Michigan. Her poem "Pickled Heads, St. Petersburg" was chosen for the 2009 edition of *Best American Poetry*.

John Reibetanz lives in Toronto and walks in its ravines. His thirteenth collection is a sequence of glosas, *Earth Words: Conversing with Three Sages* (2021); its sages are Wang An-shih, Henry Thoreau, and Emily Carr. Recent poems have appeared in *Canadian Literature, The Windsor Review*, and *Grain*.

Daniel Ricketson was a lawyer, poet, nature lover, history writer, abolitionist and friend of Henry David Thoreau. His works include *A History of New Bedford* (1858), *The Autumn Sheaf: A Collection of Miscellaneous Poems* (1869), and *Factory Bell and Other Poems* (1873).

Franklin B. Sanborn wrote memoirs about several nineteenth century transcendentalists, including Henry David Thoreau. A journalist, ardent abolitionist, and social reformer, his books include *Bronson Alcott at Alcott House, England, and Fruitlands, New England* (1842-44), *Henry D. Thoreau* (1888), *Emerson and His Friends in Concord* (1890), and *Hawthorne and His Friends: Reminiscence and Tribute* (1908).

Odell Shepard served as lieutenant governor of Connecticut and taught at Trinity College in Hartford. He wrote books on history and the outdoors. *A Lonely Flute* (1917) is a collection of poems. He won a *Pulitzer Prize* in 1938 for *Pedlar's Progress: The Life of Bronson Alcott* (1937), a biography.

Aaron Silverberg has been writing poetry since graduating in philosophy from the University of California at Santa Cruz in 1978. He is poet, photographer and personal and professional life coach. His books of poems are *Thoreau's Chair* (2001) and *Diamonds Only Water Can Wear* (2007).

Corinne H. Smith first encountered the writings of Henry David Thoreau in high school in the early 1970s. He has stayed with her, ever since. She is the author of the books, *Westward I Go Free: Tracing Thoreau's Last Journey* (2012), and *Henry David Thoreau for Kids: His Life and Ideas, With 21 Activities* (2016). She was a librarian for many years, and is also a writer and a public speaker. She is currently employed by The Thoreau Society as the Supervisor of the Shop at Walden Pond.

David Starkey served as Santa Barbara California's 2009-2011 poet laureate. He is director of the Creative Writing Program at Santa Barbara City College and the publisher and co-editor of Gunpowder Press. He has published seven full-length collections of poetry and more than 500 poems in literary journals such as *American Scholar, Georgia Review, Prairie Schooner* and *Southern Review*.

Barry Sternlieb's books of poetry include *Thinning the Rows* (1990), *Thoreau's Hat* (1994), and *Winter Crows* (2010). His work has appeared in *Poetry, Poetry Northwest, The Midwest Quarterly, Alaska Quarterly Review*, and *New England Review*.

Ingela Strandberg is a Swedish poet, novelist, author of children's books, playwright, musician and translator. Among her more than twenty-five books are the poetry collections *Lilla svarta hjärta* (*Little Black Heart*) (1999), *Bäste Herr Thoreau: Dikter* (*Dear Mr. Thoreau: Poems*) (2008), and *Den stora tystnaden vid Sirius nos* (*The Great Silence of Sirius' Nose*) (2014). Strandberg was awarded the Swedish Academy's Bellman Prize for her outstanding contribution to Swedish poetry in 2014.

Barry Targan is a novelist, short story writer, essayist, and poet. His collection of stories *Harry Belten and the Mendelssohn Violin Concerto* (1975) won the Iowa School of Letters Award for Short Fiction. Among his other books are *Falling Free* (1989), short stories, and *The Ark of the Marindor* (1998), a novel. His work has appeared in many magazines and journals including *North American Review, New Republic, Beloit Poetry Journal*, and *Shenandoah*.

Cammy Thomas' first book of poems, *Cathedral of Wish* (2005), received the 2006 Norma Farber First Book Award from the Poetry Society of America. A fellowship from the Ragdale Foundation helped her complete her second book, *Inscriptions* (2014). Her new collection, *Tremors*, arrives in 2021. She lives in Lexington, Massachusetts, and swims often in Walden Pond.

Henry David Thoreau was an essayist, poet, transcendentalist philosopher, naturalist, and environmental scientist. He is best known for his book *Walden* (1854) and his essay "Civil Disobedience."

Charles Tidler is a Canadian poet, novelist, librettist, spoken jazz artist and playwright who has written scripts for stage, radio, TV and film. Many of his poems are collected in *Straw Things: Selected Poetry & Song 1963-2007* (2008). Stage plays include *Tortoise Boy* (2004), *Rappaccini's Daughter* (2003), and *Red Mango* (2000).

Tomas Tranströmer was a leading Swedish poet of his generation, and a practicing psychologist. Among his many collections of poetry are *Windows and Stones* (1972), runner-up for the National Book Award for translation, *Sorgegondolen (Grief Gondola)* (1996), and *Den stora gåtan (The Great Enigma)* (2004). Among his many awards was the Nobel Prize in Literature for 2011.

Katharine Tynan was a widely published Irish poet and novelist with a deep interest in Celtic mythology. Active in Dublin literary circles, she wrote scores of novels and five autobiographical volumes. Her *Collected Poems* (1930) was published a year before her death.

David Wagoner has written a couple dozen volumes of poetry and ten novels. He has won two Pushcart Prizes, the Ruth Lilly Poetry Prize and other awards. *Collected Poems* (1976) and *In Broken Country* (1979) were nominated for a National Book Award.

Edmund Wilson was a leading literary critic of his time. A journalist and essayist who also wrote plays and fiction., his most famous books are *Axel's Castle: A Study in the Imaginative Literature of 1870–1930* (1931), *To the Finland Station: A Study in the Writing and Acting of History* (1940) and *Patriotic Gore: Studies in the Literature of the American Civil War* (1962).

William Butler Yeats was an Irish poet and is considered one of the greatest literary figures of the twentieth century. He won the 1923 Nobel Prize in Literature. Among his books are *Wanderings of Oisin and Other Poems* (1889) *The Countess Kathleen and Various Legends and Lyrics* (1892) *Responsibilities and* Other *Poems* (1916), and *The Winding Stair and Other Poems* (1933).

Hai Zi is the pen name of the Chinese poet Zha Haisheng who was one of the best-known poets in his country after the Cultural Revolution. Among books translated in to English are *Over Autumn Rooftops* (2010,) and *Ripened Wheat: Selected Poems of Hai Zi* (2015). He committed suicide in 1989. Thoreau's *Walden* were among the books found beside his body.

NOTES ON TEXTS AND CREDITS

A. Bronson Alcott, Sonnet XIII: *Sonnets and Canzonets* (Roberts Brothers, Boston, MA, 1882).

Louisa May Alcott, "Thoreau's Flute," from *The Atlantic Monthly* (September 1863).

Gene G. Bradbury, "Lament" from *Sauntering with Thoreau* (Book Wilde Children's Books Plus, Sequim, WA, 2014). Copyright © 2014 by Gene G. Bradbury. Reprinted with permission of the author.

J. Walter Brain, "The Loon at Walden" from *The Concord Saunterer* New Series Vol. 18 (2010). Reprinted with permission of The Thoreau Society.

William Bronk, "Flowers, the World and My Friend Thoreau" from *Life Supports: New and Collected Poems*: New Edition. Copyright © 1981 by William Bronk. Reprinted with the permission of the Rare Book and Manuscript Library, Butler Library, Columbia University.

L.M. Browning, "On the Far Side of Walden" from *Fleeting Moments of Fierce Clarity: Journal of a New England Poet* (Homebound Publications, Stonington, CT, 2012). Copyright © 2012 by Leslie M. Browning. Reprinted with permission of the author.

William Ellery Channing, "Walden" from *Poems: Second Series* (James Monroe, Boston, MA, 1847).

Ginny Lowe Connors, "Thoreau's Pumpkins." Copyright © by Ginny Lowe Connors. Printed with permission of the author.

Alison Croggon, "Sonnet: Thoreau in Chernobyl" from *New and Selected Poems 1991-2017* (Newport Street Books, Melbourne, Australia, 2017). Copyright © 2017 by Alison Croggon. Reprinted with permission of the author.

Todd Davis, "Thoreau Casts a Line in the Merrimack" from *In the Kingdom of the Ditch* (Michigan State University Press, 2013). Copyright © 2013 by Todd Davis. Reprinted with permission of the author.

Ralph Waldo Emerson, "Forbearance" from *Poems* (James Munroe & Company, Boston, MA, 1847).

Paul Engle, "Henry David Thoreau" from *Poetry* Vol. 58, No. 6 (September 1941). Reprinted with the permission of Hualing Nieh Engle.

John Enright, "Teaching Thoreau" from *Raven in Winter* (Raven Chronicles, Seattle, WA, 1994). Copyright © 1994 by John Enright. Reprinted with permission of the author

Isadore Elizabeth Flanders, "To Thoreau" from *The English Journal* (March 1929).

Robert Francis, "Thoreau in Italy" from *Collected Poems: 1936-1976* (University of Massachusetts Press, Amherst, MA, 1976). Copyright © 1976 by Robert Francis. Reprinted with permission of the University of Massachusetts Press.

Florence Kiper Frank, "Thoreau" from *The Jew to Jesus and Other Poems* (Mitchell Kennerley, New York, NY, 1915).

Parkman Howe, "Letter From Wachusett" from *Appalachia* Vol. XLVII, No. 3 (June 1991). Copyright © 1991 by Parkman Howe. The version presented here is a revision of the original. Reprinted with the permission of the author.

Donald Junkins, "July" from *Walden 100 Years After Thoreau* (Yorick Books, Boston, MA, 1969). Copyright © 1969 by Donald Junkins. Reprinted with permission of the author.

Milton Kessler, "A Good Death: For Henry David Thoreau a Century Later" from *Free Concert: New and Selected Poems* (Etruscan Press, Wilkes-Barre, PA, 2002). Copyright © 2002 by the Estate of Milton Kessler. Reprinted with the permission of The Permissions Company, LLC on behalf of Etruscan Press.

John Kinsella, "Sacred Kingfisher and Trough Filled with Water Pumped from Deep Underground" from *Jam Tree Gully* (W. W. Norton & Company, New York, 2012). Copyright © 2012 by John Kinsella. Reprinted with permission of the author.

Maxine Kumin, "Beans" from *Upcountry: Poems of New England, New and Selected* (HarperCollins, New York, NY, 1972). Copyright © 1972 by Maxine Kumin. Reprinted with permission of the Maxine Kumin Literary Trust.

David K. Leff, "Vain Strivings Untied" from *The Concord Saunterer* New Series Vol. 26 (2018). Copyright © 2018 by David K. Leff. Reprinted by permission of the author.

Timothy Liu, "Thoreau" from *Burnt Offerings* (Copper Canyon Press, Port Townsend, WA, 1995). Copyright © 1995 by Timothy Liu. Reprinted with permission of the author.

James Russell Lowell, "A Fable for Critics" from *A Fable for Critics* (G.P. Putnam, second printing, New York, NY, 1848).

Ian Marshall, "Higher Laws" from *Walden by Haiku* (The University of Georgia Press, Athens, GA, 2009). Copyright © 2009 by The University of Georgia Press. Reprinted with permission of The University of Georgia Press.

Charlie Mehrhoff, "Spring Birdlife." Copyright © 2005 by Charlie Mehrhoff. Reprinted with permission of the author.

Edward Morin, "Labor Day at Walden Pond" from *Labor Day at Walden Pond* (Ridgeway Press, Roseville, MI, 1997). Copyright © 1997 by Edward Morin. Reprinted with permission of the author.

Amy Nawrocki, "The Charity Houses of Cape Cod" from *Reconnaissance* (Homebound Publications, Stonington, CT, 2015). Copyright © 2015 by Amy Nawrocki. Reprinted with permission of the author.

Howard Nutt, "Thoreau" from *Poetry* Vol. 60, No. 2 (May 1942).

Mary Oliver, "Going to Walden" from *Devotions: The Selected Poems of Mary Oliver* (Penguin Press, New York, 2017). Copyright © 2017 by Mary Oliver. Reprinted with the permission of Regula Noetzli, Literary Agent.

Cecily Parks, "When I was Thoreau at Night" from *O'Nights*. (Alice James Books, Farmington, ME, 2015). Copyright © 2015 by Cecily Parks. Reprinted with the permission of The Permissions Company, LLC, on behalf of Alice James Books.

Janice Miller Potter, "Thoreau's Umbrella" from *Thoreau's Umbrella* (Fomite, Burlington, VT, 2019). Copyright © 2019 by Janice Miller Potter. Reprinted with permission of the author.

Susan Blackwell Ramsey, "How to Seduce Henry David Thoreau" from *A Mind Like This*. Reprinted by permission of the University of Nebraska Press. Copyright © 2012 by the Board of Regents of the University of Nebraska.

John Reibetanz, "Thoreau's Pencils" from *By Hand* (Brick Books, London, Ontario, 2019). Copyright © 2019 by John Reibetanz. Reprinted with permission of the author.

Daniel Ricketson, "Thoreau's Cairn" from *Springfield Republican* (August 13, 1872).

Franklin B. Sanborn, "Thoreau" from *The Liberator* (May 23, 1862).

Odell Shepard, "The Grave of Thoreau" from *A Lonely Flute* (Houghton Mifflin Company, Boston, MA, 1917).

Aaron Silverberg, "Thoreau's Chair" from *Thoreau's Chair: Poems* (Off the Map Enterprises, Seattle, MA, 2001) Copyright © 2001 by Aaron Silverberg. Reprinted with the permission of the author.

Corinne Hosfeld Smith, "Notes on Thoreau's Notes from Mackinac Island" from *Thoreau at Mackinac: An Anthology of Writings by Henry David Thoreau with Poetry and Prose from Mackinac Island* (Mackinac Arts Council, Mackinac Island, MI, 2017). Copyright © 2017 by Corinne Hosfeld Smith. Reprinted with the permission of the author.

David Starkey, "Allen Ginsburg in Thoreau's Maine Woods" from *Starkey's Book of States* (Boson Books, Raleigh, NC, 2008). Copyright © 2008 by David Starkey. Reprinted with permission of the author.

Barry Sternlieb, "Thoreau's Hat," reprinted from *Thoreau's Hat* (Brooding Heron Press, Waldron Island, WA, 1994). Copyright © 1994 by Barry Sternlieb. Reprinted with permission of the publisher.

Ingela Strandberg, "Dear Mr. Thoreau!" from *Dear Mr. Thoreau! Poems* (Norstedts, Stockholm, Sweden, 2008). Copyright © 2008 by Ingela Standberg. Reprinted with permission of the author. Translation by Henrik Otterberg. Used by permission.

Barry Targan, "Thoreau Stalks the Land Disguised as a Father," from *Thoreau Stalks the Land Disguised as a Father: Poems* (Greenfield Review Press, Greenfield Center, NY, 1975). Copyright © 1975 by Barry Targan. Reprinted with permission of the author.

Cammy Thomas, "Refraction" from *Inscriptions* (Four Way Books, New York, NY, 2014). Copyright © 2014 by Cammy Thomas. Reprinted with permission of Four Way Books.

Henry David Thoreau, "My life is the poem I would have writ;" "I am a parcel of vain strivings tied" from *A Week on the Concord and Merrimack Rivers* (James Monroe & Company, Boston & Cambridge, 1849).

Charles Tidler, "Transcending the Sublime Henry David" from *New American & Canadian Poetry*, edited by John Gill (Beacon Press, Boston., MA 1970). Copyright © 1970 by Charles Tidler. Reprinted with the permission of the author.

Tomas Tranströmer, "Five Stanzas for Thoreau" from *17 Poems* (Albert Bonniers förlag, Stockholm, Sweden, 1954). Copyright © 1954 by Tomas Tranströmer. Translation by Henrik Otterberg and Niklas Schiöler, originally published in *The Thoreau Society Bulletin* (Fall, 1998). Reprinted by permission of Tranströmer's estate via Monica Tranströmer, October 2020.

Katharine Tynan, "Thoreau at Walden" from *Louis de la Valliere and Other Poems* (Kegan Paul, Trench & Co., London, England, 1885).

David Wagoner, "Thoreau and the Lightning" from *After the Point of No Return*. (Copper Canyon Press, Port Townsend, WA, 2012). Copyright © 2012 by David Wagoner. Reprinted with the permission of The Permissions Company, LLC on behalf of Copper Canyon Press,

Edmund Wilson, "The Extravert of Walden Pond" from *Night Thoughts*. (Farrar, Straus & Giroux, New York, NY, 1961). Copyright © 1961 by Edmund Wilson. Reprinted with the permission of Farrar, Straus & Giroux, LLC.

William Butler Yeats "The Lake Isle of Innisfree" from *The Countess Kathleen and Various Legends and Lyrics* (T. Fisher Unwin, London, England, 1892).

Hai Zi. (Zha Haisheng), "Thoreau Has Brains," Copyright © 1986. Reprinted with the permission of the author's brother Zha Shuming through agent Lei Xia. Translation by Julia X. Du. Used by permission.

APPENDIX
*Selected Additional Poems About Thoreau**

Becker, Florence, "To Arms," from *Farewell to Walden*, Exile Press, 1939.

Black, Ralph, "Some Ants for Henry Thoreau," from Poetry Daily (www.poems.com), 2019.

Booth, Philip, "Letter from a Distant Land," from *Letter from a Distant Land*, Viking, 1957.

Carawan, William, "Visions of Thoreau while Riding the Fitchburg Line," from Words of William (www.atalethatistold.com), 2013

Carroll, Charles, "Who Freed Thoreau," typescript, Harding Collection, Thoreau Institute Library, undated.

Chute, Robert M., "Walking in The Woods with Thoreau" from *Woodshed on the Moon: Thoreau Poems*, Just Write Books, 2017.

Cimon, Anne, "Nature's Lover," typescript, Harding Collection, Thoreau Institute Library, undated.

Cosman, Max, "Homage to Thoreau," handwritten manuscript, Harding Collection, Thoreau Institute Library, undated.

Cousens, Mildred, "Even Thoreau Came Back," from *The Rotarian*, 1981.

Crowell, Reid, "Thoreau and Walden Pond," from *The Oregonian*, 1944.

Derleth, August, "Walker-Errant," from *And You, Thoreau!*, New Directions, 1944.

Dufault, Peter Kane, "Essay on Thoreau," from *For Some Stringed Instrument*, The Macmillan Company, 1957.

Engel, Dave, "Beans," from *Country Journal*, 1979.

Ferrini, Vincent, "Dialogue with Thoreau," from *The Whole Song: Selected Poems*, 2004.

Friesen, Victor Carl, "At Walden Pond," from *The Year Is a Circle: A Celebration of Henry David Thoreau*, 1995.

Gandhi, Indira, "Verse Foreword," from *Artist and Citizen Thoreau*, John J. McLeer, ed., 1971.

Goldbarth, Albert, "Henry David's Song for the Dead," from *Poetry Northwest*, 1980.

Graham, "184? or Henry in Gaol," handwritten manuscript, Harding Collection, Thoreau Institute Library, undated.

Gray, Leonard B., "Henry David Thoreau," handwritten manuscript, Harding Collection, Thoreau Institute Library, undated.

Hamilton, Robert L., "Old Concord Voices Speak on Author's Ridge," typescript, Harding Collection, Thoreau Institute Library, 1950.

Hannan, Dennis J. "There was a Young Thoreau Named Henry," typescript, Harding Collection, Thoreau Institute Library, undated.

Herbelein, Larry, "Thoreau at a Party," from *South Dakota Review*, 1984.

Heinle, Charles A. S., "Wild Man of Walden," typescript, Harding Collection, Thoreau Institute Library, undated.

Higginson, Storrow, "Henry D. Thoreau," from *In Memory of Henry D. Thoreau*, Ysleta, Edwin B. Hill, 1944.

Hooper, Peter, "A Leaf for Thoreau," from *Mushroom*, 1978.

Howe, Susan, "Thorow," from *Singularities*, Wesleyan University Press, 1990.

Jones, Samuel A., "Thoreau," from *In Memory of Henry D. Thoreau*, Ysleta, Edwin B. Hill, 1944.

Jorgenson, M. A., "The Gentle Man of Concord," typescript, Harding Collection, Thoreau Institute Library, undated.

Kempof, Joseph H., "A Letter to Henry David Thoreau," *Sewanee Review*, 1975.

Kempa, Rick, "Triptych for Thoreau," *The Concord Saunterer*, 2016.
Kennedy, Mary, "In Search of Thoreau and Emerson," from *Ride into Morning*, Gotham Book Mart, 1969.

Kerns, Ida M. "Thoreau," from *In Memory of Henry D. Thoreau*, Ysleta, Edwin B. Hill, 1944.

Keyes, Langley Carleton, "Thoreau," from *Thoreau: Voice in the Edgeland*, University of North Carolina Press, 1955.

Leigh, Betty, "Concord Meadows (Remembering Thoreau)," from *The Friendly Quill*, 1942.

Levesque, Andy, "Walden Vision Quest," from *Walden Vision Quest and Other Poems*, self-published chapbook, 1995.

McCarthy, Mary, "H.D. Thoreau and the Echoes," typescript, Harding Collection, Thoreau Institute Library, undated.

McNally, Peter, "Coming to terms with Henry David Thoreau on a Sunday Morning in January of 1973," from *American Transcendental Quarterly*, 1974.

Millard, Bailey, "Thoreau of Walden," from *In Memory of Henry D. Thoreau*, Ysleta, Edwin B. Hill, 1944.

Owen, Riverdave, "The Border Life," www.theborderlife.com, 2012.

Petrie, Paul, "Thoreau," from *Christian Century*, 1986.

Pettigrew, Richard C., "Thoreau," from *The Poetry Chap-Book*, 1949.
Scott, Louise, "And a Small Cabin Built There," from *Educational Forum*, 1962.

Seaburg, Alan, *Thoreau Collage*, Privately Printed, 1978.

Simpson, Julia Meylor, "On Pondering Thoreau's Ants," from *Tiferet Journal*, 2018.

Staples, Catherine, "Dear Henry," from *The Southern Review*, 2018.

Steffen, Michael, "Concord," from *The Concord Saunterer*, 2019.

Stevens, Peter, "Magpies and Thoreau," from *Cottonwood Review*, 1969.

Stott, Sandy, "Declaration," from *The Roost*, www.thoreaufarm.org, 2015.

Strier, Richard, "Purity at Walden," from *Chicago Review*, 1975.

Tarrant, Desmond, "Henry David Thoreau," from *Kaleidograph*, 1949.

Teare, Brian, "This book can't be sung (Reading Walden)," from *Boston Review*, 2007.

Thomas, Isabel, "The Ghost of Walden," typescript, Harding Collection, Thoreau Institute Library, 1968.

Yasinski, Nick, "Swimming in Walden," from *Virginia Literary Review*, 1989.

* *This list excludes poets with a poem printed in this volume. Although many poets have multiple poems about Thoreau, only one poem per poet is included.*

ABOUT THE EDITOR

David K. Leff is an award-winning poet and essayist, and former deputy commissioner of the Connecticut Department of Environmental Protection. He is the Canton, Connecticut poet laureate, deputy town historian, and town meeting moderator. He was a volunteer firefighter for 26 years.

In 2016 and 2017 David was appointed by the National Park Service to serve as poet-in-residence for the New England National Scenic Trail (NET). He has been nominated three times for a Pushcart Prize, and has twice been a finalist in the Connecticut Book Awards. David has received two silver medals from the Independent Publisher Book Awards (IPPY), and was grand prize short-listed for the Eric Hoffer Book Award. His work has appeared in anthologies, newspapers such as the *Hartford Courant*, and magazines including *Appalachia* and *Yankee*.

The author of seven nonfiction books, three volumes of poetry, and two novels in verse, David's work focuses on the connection of people to their communities and the natural environment. He often explores commonplace elements of the world around us that have hidden meanings and unusual links to each other.

David has been the book review editor of Connecticut Woodlands, the quarterly magazine of the Connecticut Forest & Park Association and is now poetry editor. He is a staff writer for *The Wayfarer Magazine*.

David's papers are located at the
Special Collections and University Archives, UMass/Amherst.
View his work at www.davidkleff.com

HOMEBOUND
PUBLICATIONS

We are an award-winning independent publisher founded in 2011 striving to ensure that the mainstream is not the only stream. More than a company, we are a community of writers and readers exploring the larger questions we face as a global village. It is our intention to preserve contemplative storytelling. We publish full-length introspective works of creative non-fiction, literary fiction, and poetry.

WWW.HOMEBOUNDPUBLICATIONS.COM

www.ingramcontent.com/pod-product-compliance
Lightning Source LLC
Chambersburg PA
CBHW020423010526
44118CB00010B/391